Bright Ideas Lifesavers

Written by Diane Montgomery, Anne Rawlings, Norma Hadfield

Contents

Published by Scholastic Publications Ltd,
Marlborough House, Holly Walk,
Leamington Spa, Warwickshire CV32 4LS.

© 1987 Scholastic Publications Ltd

Written by Diane Montgomery,
Anne Rawlings and
Norma Hadfield
Edited by Philip Steele
Sub-edited by Jackie Cunningham-Craig
Illustrations by Ken Stott

Printed in Great Britain by
Loxley Brothers Ltd, Sheffield

ISBN 0 590 706942

Front and back cover: Martyn Chillmaid

Introduction

Bright Ideas Lifesavers is the answer to every teacher's dream – a comprehensive guide to activities, lessons and projects for those times when they need, at their fingertips, instant ideas to make the school day run more smoothly. Busy teachers will find the large section of photocopiable material particularly useful. We have also provided a compendium of useful addresses and contacts which any teacher will find an invaluable source of information.

BEGINNING OF TERM
This chapter is jam-packed with ideas, tips and activities for beginning a term – not only for the old regular pupils beginning a new year but also for those starting school for the very first time. Many lively activities have been given so that both parties can soon get to know each other and establish a good working relationship.

FIVE MINUTE FILLERS
There are always those little patches in the school day where a session has finished quickly and you need to fill the time in a useful and, if possible, educationally productive way. Five minute fillers has a number of these 'extras'. They are suggestions designed as a starting point which can be expanded, in many cases, to fill the five minutes which often become ten when the bell is late.

Sometimes, it is only individual children who have finished quickly and need something useful to do, so that they do not annoy other children. These are indicated by the group size eg individual or pairs. However, some will require advance preparation or materials which are not available for the whole class. It is immensely helpful to have a collection of these 'filler kits' in your classroom which can be brought out as necessary. Often, you will find the children enjoy the fillers so much they want to carry on working on them, or they lead to whole new lessons later in the day.

Very able children often finish work before the others and so we have included some mental gymnastic problems, such as Link's cube and the Brahma Tower, which even adults find difficult.

Games such as Categories, Word crocodiles, Main talking points, Butchers and bakers, Diagrams, Draw a face, Anagrams, Test your memory, and Words within words, require no preparation and can be used with any sized group.

Dictionary skills, Kim's games, Telephone directory scanning, and Counters, need the minimum of preparation. Mostly, the teacher will just need to check that particular items are available or make a quick collection of them.

Stick it in, Counting, Dog biscuits, Snowmen, Sort and post, Paper flowers, and One-fold fun all require the teacher to make a 'kit' in advance and hold in readiness. Our suggestions are merely starters to get you going.

INSTANT LESSONS
Here we provide a range of lessons to suit different needs. Lessons for that time when there is suddenly half an hour, or an hour, to fill with someone else's class. Sessions for which you have no time to prepare but just pick up *Lifesavers* and teach.

The first half of this chapter is filled with lessons that involve talking, reading, and writing. The second half involves painting, printing and making. We have assumed that nearly every primary classroom has scissors, paints, brushes, newspapers and collage oddments to hand. All that is necessary is for the teacher to organise the children to collect and layout the necessary items. In addition, it is especially important, even when using one-off lessons such as these, to try to incorporate the elements of problem solving into a pattern of work, with always a follow-up or concluding discussion on the effectiveness of what has been produced in visual terms.

You will notice that many of the lessons involve the children working in groups and talking about what they are going to do. This is very important for them, for they often do not know what they think until they have explained it to someone else.

PENCIL AND PAPER ACTIVITIES
A series of pencil and paper activities have been designed which can either be lifted straight from the page and used directly in the classroom, or the relevant copy page can

be photocopied and used.

During paper and pencil activities, make sure that the less able children are catered for by using the activities in a flexible way. For example, if reading skills are poor, arrange for pairs to work on Friendly words. In any case, some activities, such as Alphabet poems, are usually arranged for pairs. Some children may have satisfactory reading skills but have difficulties in handwriting co-ordination. They may need a friend to do the recording for them, or with them. Where feasible, the lessons are structured so that talking about the tasks is legitimised, and becomes part of the on-going programme.

OUTDOOR ACTIVITIES

Outdoor activities are often a neglected area, mainly due to weather conditions in this country, so when the sun shines use the opportunity to take the children outside. On colder days, winter warm-up games such as Traffic lights, Tag games, In the sea, and the Compass game, are ideal. Snow detectives, Shadow images, and Colour kite are examples of using weather phenomena in a constructive problem-solving way. Nature map, Litter studies and Stars boxes are preliminary exploratory studies to open up scientific and environmental problem-solving pursuits. Individual children or groups often like to continue these studies as projects on natural history, pollution and astronomy, and can become quite expert in these areas. Children can go on to design further experiments and projects in which you, and the whole class, can participate.

The Statues game, Compasses, and In the sea require skills such as looking and listening, moving to cue, and being still. Statues, in particular, can be used when it is important for the children to be well under control and quiet. Establish the rules before going out of the classroom, especially on windy days, when your voice may not be heard clearly!

Beginning of term

For teachers and others who manage children in groups, one of the most important moments is when all are gathered together for the first encounter. Most people feel shy and self-conscious in an environment which they are not used to. The aim must be to create a positive, friendly and secure atmosphere, in which the group can feel free to put forward ideas and communicate without fear of feeling foolish. To achieve this, it is necessary to take certain steps. The sequence suggested is as follows: organisation → the welcome → the initial introduction → establishing the rules → the events → evaluation.

These six steps encapsulate a strategy for success. Good relationships and a learning environment are built on self-confidence, the ability to communicate and co-operation.

Organisation

Planning and preparation demand as much time, if not more, than the activities themselves. The first impressions children have of a new class or situation can be long-lasting; some children carry their fears and worries with them long into their school careers. Because of this, it is essential to make the transition from home, school, class or new school as smooth as possible, both for the child and for the teacher or adult responsible. If possible try to see the new group of children for a short time before the start of the new term or the change. This will give both parties a chance to get to know one another.

Learning the child's name in the first instance is of paramount importance. It makes the child feel valued and important. Get a list of names, and find out if they are actually called by these names. It may be they prefer a shortened version, or some nickname. Look for some distinguishing feature, such as a mole, hair colour, shape of face, or colour of eyes to help you remember the name. Don't go by clothing, as this can change!

Try to have the room already set up on the first day. Choose activities which do not require a great deal of clearing away. Otherwise you will find the evening taken up with this chore, as the children will not yet know how the classroom is organised.

The welcome

For nursery or infant classes, try to prepare in advance a name card with a picture on it. If possible, prepare matching pictures for the coat peg, the lunch-box tray etc. This will help the younger children to feel that they belong. The picture can be 'portable', if not enough pictures can be found for each child.

For older children, prepare a set of envelopes containing 'a secret'. These can be given away at playtime. They will help to break the ice and give them something to look forward to.

Try to stand at the door and welcome children in with a smile. Tell them where you want them to sit and what you want them to do. This will make them feel more at ease. Younger children may need help with buttons, coat etc. Try to have another pair of hands available on that first day.

The initial introduction

As soon as everyone is gathered together, gain quietness, and then state who you are: 'I am . . . your teacher/play leader/helper and I will be helping to look after you for the next . . . . We are going to have some fun and spend the next few minutes getting to know each other a little better.' Then play some simple 'getting to know you' games. This will help to give a sense of identity and personal contact.

Establishing the rules

Do not give out a long list of rules on the first day. Just try to establish how you can quieten the group as quickly as possible. Let children know that they can go to the toilet as long as they ask you first. Caution: on the first day, unless the toilets are attached to the classroom, children can become nervous about finding their way there and back. Other children may take the opportunity to search for mum! During the course of the morning do several head counts, just in case.

The events

Talk through the events of the morning, so that the children know the type of activity that is going to take place. This helps to allay fears children may have that they are expected to read, write and do complicated number work all in the first few hours! For older children, a day's agenda is particularly useful, as it encourages a feeling of autonomy and participation. The agenda can also serve as a record of their first day in the new environment, and as a work sheet. Make sure the agenda includes playtimes, assemblies etc.

name cards

Evaluation

To finish the morning or day with an evaluation is important even with younger children. It helps to make the children feel that their ideas and comments are valued and worthwhile. It also acts as a record of what the children found enjoyable/useful/exciting/boring/difficult. This helps the adult responsible to make amendments and to decide on future agendas. Once the older children have gained trust and self-confidence they might at some future time be invited to assess how well they performed. Always encourage them to put the positive side first: 'something you did really well'. Children with special needs require help in recognising their achievements.

The aim should be to provide a supportive atmosphere where children can be honest about themselves without being 'put down'. They must know that they will be listened to and understood.

Getting to know you 1

Age range
Five to ten.

Group size
Whole class.

sticky label

What you need
Plenty of sticky labels large enough to write names and draw a picture on, felt pens, a few sheets of paper to give out for those who need to copy.

What to do
Ask the children to write their names on a sticky label, and to draw something on the label which they like. Encourage the children to write their names clearly and large enough for others to read. Move quickly round the class to identify those children who cannot write their names as yet. Go back to them and help them. Encourage them to copy out their name if possible.

9

Knotty fun

Age range
Five to eight.

Group size
Whole class.

What you need
Lots of old jumpers which have been tied into knots.

What to do
In this game, jumpers are thrown from one child to another. The first time the game is played, it is better if one jumper is thrown to a child who calls out his or her own name on catching it. Subsequently, the children call out the name of the child to whom they are going to throw the jumper. The object of the game is to try to keep as many jumpers going as possible. The record so far is five! This game is a good 'ice breaker' and always popular with children.

Getting to know you 2 and 3

Age range
Five to thirteen.

Group size
Whole class.

What to do
Sit in a circle. Explain to the children that they have to say what their name is, and two more things about themselves. You begin 'My name is . . . and I like chocolate and going skiing'. When everyone in the class has completed this, see how many names you can remember and how many they can. Go round again . . .

Age range
Five to thirteen.

Group size
Small group or whole class.

What you need
A hat or a brick or a newspaper.

What to do
Take an everyday object and show it to the group. Explain that the idea is to think up unusual ways of using it. A hat or indeed anything you have to hand will do. You start off: 'My name is . . . and I *sat* on it' – and so on. To break the ice, encourage ingenious and comical ideas as well as more ordinary ones. Praise everyone who joins in.

Listening and telling

Age range
Seven to thirteen.

Group size
Pairs in small groups of six
or pairs within the whole class.

What to do
Arrange the pupils in pairs. Let them choose friends as partners, or simply work with the person next to them, whichever is most convenient. Spread the pairs out as far from each other as possible.

Explain one of the most important things that they are going to learn now they are in the new school or class is that they will need to *listen* in order to learn. Discuss the possibility that people do not always really listen to what they are told. Explain how they sometimes do the wrong things or the opposite of what they were told to do. Ask if they have any examples of this.

Explain in simple terms what adults call the 'party syndrome'. This is the tendency we all have to hear our own name even when there is a lot of other noise, although we do not hear much else. Ask the children to notice this. Stress the importance of learning people's names so that you can get their attention.

The pairs of pupils should sit opposite each other and take turns in telling their partner who they are and something about themselves. Younger groups can take 30 seconds each. Older groups can take one minute each. After the first of the pair has told about themselves, all the partners then tell the class or group how much they can remember of what they heard. Those who have to wait for their turn will tend to forget, so allow their partner to prompt them a little.

After all the characters have been introduced allow them to swap roles, so that the speakers have to listen to their partners and then tell the group in their turn.

The teacher could if necessary break a large class group into three or four autonomous groups. Avoid this where possible, for in the standard group a lot can be learned about the pupils' forthcomingness and language facility.

Some children will be too shy to say anything. In the youngest groups some will be too immature to follow what to do. Others will explain about themselves rather than their partners. Be sensitive. Quickly transfer them to another activity.

Make quick notes in your records about each pupil's performance. This activity provides a preliminary screening of language and personal/social development, which can be very useful. Note any difficulties in speech, articulation or behaviour.

The exercise is a good way of making friends for children who are meeting for the first time.

Unusual words

Age range
Eight to thirteen.

Group size
Groups of four.

What you need
One dictionary per small group,
paper, pencil,
collection of unusual words.

an Indian snake which is very dangerous

cobra

What to do
The person with the dictionary chooses an unusual word. The next person considers the meaning of that word and writes it down. They fold it over and hand it to the next person, who draws a picture. The last person in the group opens up the paper and tries to give the meaning of the word from the picture and word clues.

Lettergrams

Age range
Five to thirteen.

Group size
Small groups.

What you need
Card, paper,
letters of the alphabet (on small cards),
carrier bags, pencils.

What to do
Put the letters of the alphabet into carrier bags. Prepare cards with subjects written or drawn on them. Examples might include birthdays, a visit, a wedding, excuses for missing a bus or a lesson etc. The cards should be put in a large envelope. Each group will need its own envelope and bag of letters.

Participants pull 12 letter cards out of the bag, and one subject card out of the envelope. Each player notes down his or her letters and subject, and then puts them back. The bag and envelope is then passed on. Each player must then write a message of 12 words. Each word must start with the letters in the same sequence as they were pulled out of the bag: eg ISTBLMNTBFAW might be made into:

'I'm sorry to be late, my Nan took Ben for a walk'.

There are many variations to this game. For children in the *five to seven* age range, the groups should be smaller and work co–operatively. Each player pulls just one letter from the bag, and provides one word towards the group's final sentence.

Picturegrams

Age range
Three to six.

Group size
Groups of three.

What you need
Cards,
envelopes,
old magazines
(optional),
old comics
(for older pupils).

What to do
Draw on to cards sets of three pictures in which a sequence of events is shown. Subjects might include a candle burning down, a cake being eaten, a bridge being raised, a dog running off with a bone, a football being kicked and breaking a window. Alternatively, cut out sets of three magazine pictures which can be put together to make up a story. Place the cards in an envelope.

The children each draw out a picture. They decide which one is to tell the first bit of the story. He or she lines up first in their group, facing the other two. The group then sorts out who goes second and third, and how they will tell their story.

NB If teachers wish to save time they can give one group of pupils comic strips and scissors. They code them on the back or record them secretly, then cut them up and pass them on to a second group, who must sort out the correct order and check with the first group.

Pirates

Age range
Three to seven.

Group size
Small or whole class.

What you need
Lots of items for 'treasure',
scarf as a blindfold.

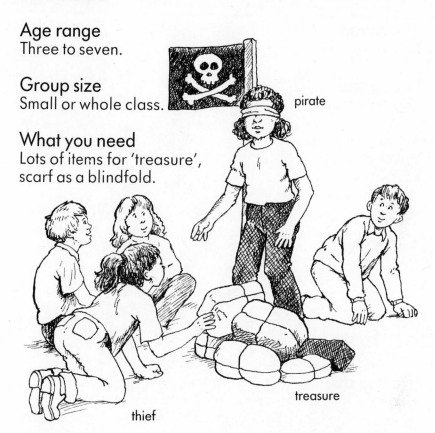

pirate

treasure

thief

What to do
One player sits blindfolded in the middle of the 'treasure'. Players sit in a large circle around this 'pirate'. The teacher then points to one of the players in the circle, who must creep very quietly to take a piece of treasure. The pirate listens very carefully for the 'thief', and should try to point in their direction. If the pirate points directly at the thief, he or she can then become the pirate in the middle, and another player is chosen as thief. This continues until all the treasure is stolen.

Whispers

Age range
Five to ten.

Group size
Small group
or teams.

What you need
Sentences to whisper
(see copy page 101
for suggestions).

What to do
Either: Sit the pupils in a circle. The beginner whispers a
sentence into his or her neighbour's ear so it is passed on
round the whole group. The last one has to say the
sentence out loud. The original sentence is then read out,
usually amidst laughter!

Or: In a larger space, spread out the teams and call the
leaders to you. Show them the sentence or say it to them.
They then go back to their teams and on the word 'go!'
whisper the sentence to their team mate. The sentence is
passed on down the line. The last one runs to you and
writes down what he or she thinks is the sentence! The
team who comes closest to the original sentence wins.

Mime a picture

Age range
Three to eight.

Group size
Small groups
or whole class.

What you need
Old catalogues
and magazines,
scissors,
glue,
stiff card,
shoe box.

What to do
Cut out all kinds of pictures from old catalogues and
magazines. Stick them on to stiff card, and place them in
a shoe box.
  Invite the children to put their hand into the box one at a
time. They should then study the picture and mime the
object to the rest. Other players must guess what is on the
picture. Do not force any child to do the mime who does
not want to. Some just enjoy watching at first. This is
another good way to get to know different children.
Some who shine at this activity fail when it comes to
drawing and writing. Watch out for these children, as
they will need your special support and encouragement.

Sorting pictures

Age range
Three to six.

Group size
Small groups
or whole class.

What you need
Source of pictures,
scissors, glue, stiff
card, shoe box.

What to do
Prepare boxes of pictures of objects as before, with at
least 20–30 pictures per box. Theme magazines on
animals, boats, cars etc are a very useful source of
material, as are used postcards and photographs.

Pupils are placed in small groups. They are not told
what to sort for, but simply asked to decide which
pictures belong with which. When they have sorted
through them once, they should write down a title for
each category sorted. They should then take two of these
categories and try to re-sort them into smaller sub-
categories. This activity increases their powers of
observation of pictures. It encourages analysis and
mental processing in concept development. It also
enables the children to discuss (and, if they are able, to
record) what they have done in their own words. The
teacher should listen in to these discussions and look at
the records the children have made. Many clues are
available which will help diagnose learning needs and
assess with what literacy skills the pupils have arrived in
the classroom.

Hello hello!

Age range
Eight to thirteen.

Group size
Small or large groups.

What you need
Pencil,
'discovery sheet'.

What to do
A good way for people to get to know each other is by
carrying out a survey. The children carrying out the
survey should talk to as many people as possible, and
find out all they can. The results can be recorded on a
'discovery sheet'. When planning a discovery sheet,
make sure that most people will qualify for inclusion.

Who . . .
Has lived in ..... all his/her life? ....
Ran in a mini-marathon? ....
Has a favourite radio/TV programme? ....
Has an unusual hobby? ....
Has cooked a meal? ....
Likes gardening? ....
Has won a raffle or prize? ....
Has read a good book lately? ....
Has been on television? ....
Has had an accident? ....
Does not like sport? ....
Was born abroad? ....
Plays a musical instrument? ....
Has slept in a tent? ....

Number puzzles: totals

Age range
Six to ten.

Group size
Individuals,
pairs,
or whole class.

What you need
Copy page 102,
pencils.

What to do
Give out the copies of page 102, one per pupil or, if
working in pairs, one between two. Explain how to do the
worked examples as follows.

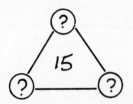 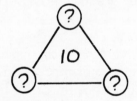

- What numbers must be put in the three circles to add
  up to 15? Use only numbers 1 to 9 eg 4,9,2,(=15).
  The numbers 1 to 9 may only be used once.
- How many triangle sums to 10 can anyone make?

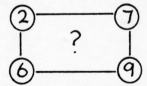

- What is the total score to put in the square? The
  answer here would be 24.

Number puzzles: sides

Age range
Eight to thirteen.

Group size
Individuals,
pairs,
or whole class.

What you need
Copy page 103,
pencils.

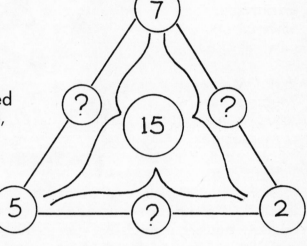

What to do
Give out copies of page 103, one per pupil or, if working
in pairs, one between two. Explain how to do the puzzle
by giving an example. Each of the *side* lines of this
triangle must add up to 15. Use only numbers 1–9. If the
pupils cannot do the sums in their heads, show them how
the sums can be written down:

$$5 + 7 + ? = 15$$

Any numbers below 13 can be put in the first circle.
Start off, using the lowest numbers first. The second
number must be one which will not make the sum so far
add up to more than 14, so that the sequence can at least
be completed with 1.

Crossnumbers

Age range
Six to thirteen

Group size
Individuals,
pairs,
class.

What you need
Copy pages 104–5,
pencils.

puzzle

Answers

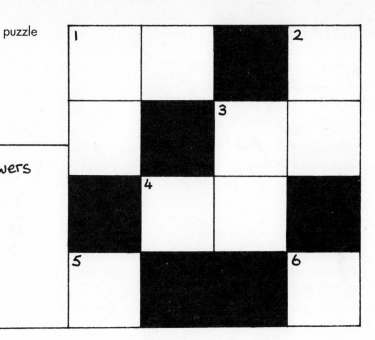

What to do

This is another way of practising and consolidating number skills that have been learnt. Explain that a crossnumber is like a crossword. Work through the example with the class to make sure they understand. It is easy to copy whichever crossword blank is suitable for your pupils, and to change the clues to make the sums: tens and units; hundreds, tens and units; addition only; addition and subtraction only; multiplication to six; mixed skills and so on.

Put this blank example on the board with the following clues:

Clues

Across
1 $(6 + 6)$
3 (5×5)
4 (4×12)
5 $(15 - 6)$
6 $(8 \div 2)$
or eg (2×2)

Down
1 (3×6)
2 (5×3)
3 $(10 + 10 + 8)$

Follow-up

A variety of this is to get the children to fill in their own clues. A difficult example is given on copy page 105. The teacher just has to fill in the simpler crossnumber blanks and delete the clues. This provides a different exercise for the pupils to do, which will help to consolidate number work.

Talking points

Age range
Five to thirteen.

Group size
Small groups of six or eight or whole class.

What you need
A3 size paper
glue, scissors,
postcards or
old magazines,
photocopying facility.

Robber chased

A BRAVE Rugby woman frightened off a thief who snatched £20 from the till at her Manor Road shop on Thursday evening.

Gupreet Sandhu was working in the Takhar Stores when a man entered the shop just

But when Mrs Sandhu opened the cash till he reached over the counter and grabbed £20 from the open till.

Quick-thinking Mrs Sandhu grabbed a six inch knife from behind the counter and the raider ran out of the shop. She was not hurt in the theft.

The thief is described as six feet tall, 20 to 22 years old and

What to do
Select six pictures from the previous sessions on mime or picture sorting and stick them on to the A3 paper. Try to choose pictures which will stimulate discussion; postcards are most useful. Number the pictures. Make enough copies for one between two children in each of the groups (eg three or four copies per group).

Ask each group to choose first of all the picture which they like the most, on an individual basis. Each person in the group must then say why they like that particular picture. The second task is for the group to choose which picture they prefer as a group. This will involve the children in negotiation and discussion. If a group cannot decide on which picture they prefer, ask each group how they can solve the dilemma. A vote can be taken. At this stage, when the groups have chosen as individuals and as groups, then all the groups could be gathered together and asked to decide on a picture to represent the whole class. This activity helps to stimulate discussion, and helps the children to negotiate and find answers to solutions together. It also allows the adults working with the groups to encourage discussion and reading.

Abandoned pets: there are too many dogs

Follow-up
For *younger children* fewer cards could be used. To extend this activity for *older children* use controversial articles or pictures from newspapers or magazines.

Follow me

Age range
Three to seven.

Group size
Whole class
or small group.

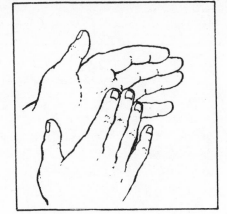

1 rubbing hands:
a gentle wind

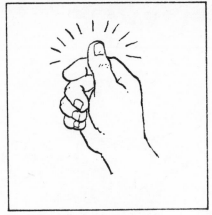

2 clicking fingers:
raindrops

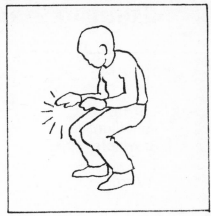

3 patting knees:
heavy rain

What to do

Decide on a sequence of events or actions which the children have to follow. The children should sit in a large circle while the teacher stands in the middle. A favourite sequence which younger children enjoy is the coming of a storm. Go to each child in turn and start to 'build up' the storm. Start by gently rubbing hands together. Children follow your actions round the circle, one after another as you come to them. They must keep rubbing until you come to them again. At the same time talk about how first of all the wind gently blows through the leaves, shaking and rustling them. As you come back to the first child the next action is to click fingers. Explain that this is the raindrops dropping on the leaves, and that soon the rain will be falling heavily. As you come round the circle to the first child, pat your knees: this is the heavy rain. Now it looks like thunder: stamp your feet. As you come round again to the first child, do the actions in reverse order, until all the thunder, rain and wind has stopped, and the day is sunny and warm. This activity is excellent for gaining quiet after a busy morning.

Other events could be used such as a battle, a swim, going for a walk or a bike ride.

4 stamping:
thunder

19

Creative gardens

Age range
Three to five.

Group size
Individuals
or small groups.

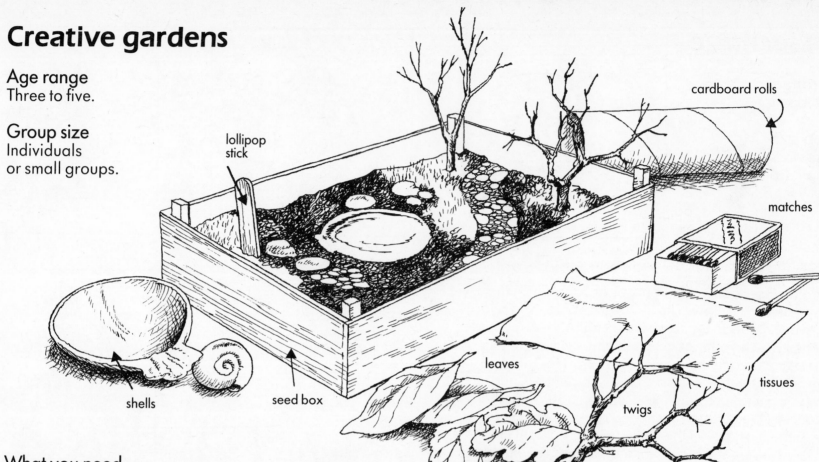

What you need
Empty trays, such as seed trays or shallow polystyrene
trays. Selection of different materials – used matches,
shells, lollipop sticks, straws, twigs, milk bottle tops,
tissue, leaves, pebbles, cardboard tubes.

What to do
Fill the tray with some damp sand and press down firmly.
Let the children design their own garden with the
materials. This type of activity can be therapeutic for
children who are upset. After designing their garden,
they can then tell others what they have made.

Follow-up
The children could be taken for a walk in the school
grounds with an adult, to collect pieces for their 'garden'.
If the children are new to school this helps them to
familiarise themselves with the school grounds. They
could be encouraged to notice where they find things: is it
under a bush, a tree and so on? This helps to develop
their powers of observation and encourages an eye for
detail. A display could be made of the gardens, or they
could be taken home!

Just imagine

Age range
Three to nine.

Group size
Groups of six to eight.

What you need
Selection of materials, paper, scissors, glue, coloured tissue, stapler, a large envelope for each group, pieces of paper, felt pens, a selection of four or five different types of flowers. Try to choose flowers that have different attributes, eg hairy stem, pointed leaves, textured leaves, drooping head.

What to do
Cover each work surface with newspaper. Put a selection of the different materials on each table. For younger children, prepare some phrases describing the parts of a flower, eg 'twisty stalk', 'spiky leaves', 'fat root', 'hairy stem'. Place as many descriptions as you can think of in each envelope and hand out one to each group.

First of all show the children your real flowers, and talk about their various points. Divide the children into groups and explain that they are going to make imaginary flowers together. Each child pulls out of the envelope a description of part of the flower. It does not matter if the parts they pull out do not make a complete flower.

Older children could decide which parts they want to put on the pieces of paper in the large envelope. This helps the children to discuss parts of a flower, and also encourages them to use descriptive language.

Each individual has to make their part of the flower from the selection of materials provided. When each child has done this the whole group decides how the parts will be put together to make a complete imaginary flower. This activity can often lead on to poems and writing. It can also be applied to other imaginary items such as monsters, people, places and houses.

Birthday line-up

Age range
Seven to thirteen.

Group size
Whole class.

What to do
Make sure that the pupils know the dates of their own birthdays. Ask them to line up in birthday order.

Follow-up
For *older children* ask them to separate into groups that add up as nearly as possible to 100, when considering the day of the month on which they were born (eg 1st, 2nd, 3rd, 4th).

Reading session

Age range
Five to thirteen.

Group size
Individuals.

What you need
Children's reading books.

What to do
Set aside the period after lunch every day in order to settle the children down. They should get out their reading books and silently read for 10 to 20 minutes, depending on age and typical concentration span. If you establish such a period, it gives children time to digest their lunch. It also allows them to cool and calm down after the excitements of a long playtime. This is a period when they are ready to rest and concentrate. After a time they will know the routine and come in quietly. They will get out their books and begin without being made to. In this period the teacher can hear individuals read without interruption, and help them with their progress.

This kind of quiet time is often rare in a busy school day. Sometimes teachers could read a book themselves, and set an example.

'Our first week' folder

Age range
Eight to thirteen.

Group size
Whole class.

What you need
Folders,
paper,
coloured felt-tip pens.

What to do
This activity is ideal for children on their first day in a new school. Provide a folder for each new pupil, with the name of the school written in large letters on the front. If the school has a coat of arms this should also be on the cover. The letters and coat of arms should be large enough to be coloured in and decorated. Inside the folders there should be sheets of paper. Page one should be blank. Page two consists of a copy of the timetable, or a blank version which you fill in together. Page three can be a general map of the school. Pages four, five and six should be blank.

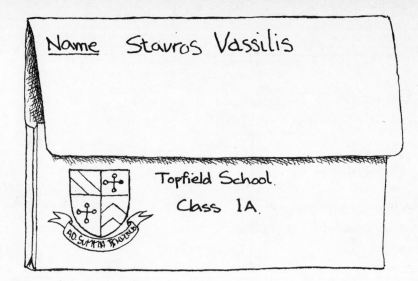

Cover
Give out the folder and ask the pupils to write their name on the front cover.

Discuss the school colours, if there are any. Suggest that the pupils decorate their front cover using these colours. They could also decorate it with some personal motif, such as their initials, in colours of their own choice.

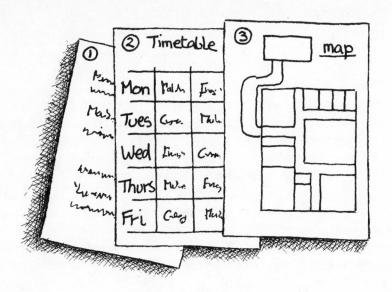

Page one

First the pupils should write down the name and address of the school and its telephone number. They should list the names of the headteacher, the secretary and the caretaker. At the bottom of page one they should write their own name, address and telephone number if any.

Ask if any one knows how the school came to get its name. What is significant about it? Is it named after someone, eg Benjamin Britten School? Does the name have a special meaning for people in the area? Does it describe a location, eg Green Lane or Tolworth? It might be interesting to find out the origin of such place names.

Tell the pupils the history of the school in brief. Suggest they note down any key points on their page one.

Page two

The pupils should have the timetable or the pattern of the day, and subjects or areas of study, explained to them. They should make a note of their class teacher's name, and that of any other helpers or teachers.

Page three

The general map of the new school is very important in this first week. Suggest that the pupils colour in the rooms on their maps to help find their way about. Lavatories are important, and should have their own special colour. So should the home base or classroom, halls and gymnasia, administration and medical rooms.

When they have completed colouring in their maps, and made a colour key, ask them to work out how to get from the classroom to the playground for break. If this is just outside the classroom door, plan suitable expeditions to other locations during the day – but not one after the other. Groups of three could be sent on an expedition to the secretary, for example, to receive her signature to say they arrived. Senior pupils in the school could be asked to accompany these small groups. They should not lead them, but just make sure that all is well.

When the trips are complete, gather the class together and let them tell you and each other how they got on.

Pages four to six

If the school has a homework pattern, then this can be recorded on page four with times, to show parents what might be expected.

On page five the children can add anything more they discover about the school, its past pupils, or important school events.

Page six should be completed on the first Friday. Encourage the children to write down their thoughts and describe their experiences during their first week in the new school.

Class books 1

Age range
Six to thirteen.

Group size
Whole class.

What you need
Snapshots,
scrap paper,
paper,
felt-tip pens.

What to do

Ask everyone to bring a snapshot of themselves, use an official school photograph, or else take pictures of children yourself. Failing this, a drawing by the child of him or herself will do.

Position the photo or drawing on a sheet of paper and draw round it. On scrap paper, the class write about their family, home, pets, hobbies etc. When they have finished you can discuss how to arrange the material on the sheet, with some small illustrations. The pages are then collected together in a book called 'Our Class' which can be used for discussion or for reading. It is very useful for new members of the class to read. The children will be very proud of their book. It will be very helpful in bringing together a class in a joint effort, particularly when there are children of several ages.

Name: Helen Williams
Birthday: 17 May 1979
Home: 33 Durham Road
Berwick

Pets: 1 Hamster
Hobbies: Riding

Our Class
3G

Class books 2

Age range
Six to thirteen.

Group size
Whole class or
small groups.

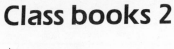

photo album

What you need
Cheap photograph album (the kind with plastic film laid
over the photographs), paper.

What to do
Take photographs on outings, of special events, during
drama productions etc. Discuss with the children which
are the best ones, and the best order to put them in.
Younger children can then write captions, and older
children a longer piece of writing. These can be placed
below the photographs.

These albums are very useful in the book corner and
are referred to frequently by the children. They also
provide a more permanent record of the year's activities
than a wall display. Although this is not a cheap activity
the pride and interest stimulated is considerable.

Class books 3

Age range
Five to thirteen.

Group size
Small groups
or whole class.

What you need
Paper,
glue or
stapler
or needle and thread,
scissors,
string.

What to do
Collect class drawings, poems and stories. Mount them
on a number of sheets which you can glue, stitch or staple
together. Ask the children to suggest what shape the
book should be and ways of decorating covers. The
pages inside can be rectangular or all cut in some special
shape.

Display the books on shelves or by hanging them up
with string loops. A small group working on a topic might
enjoy producing a book for the rest of the class. In this
way you could build up a collection.

Five minute fillers

Categories

Age range
Eight to thirteen.

Group size
Individuals,
small groups or whole class.

What you need
Paper,
pencil.

table

Category	H	A	N	D	S
Animal	horse	ant			
Place	Hackney				
Name	Harry				
Food	ham				
Country.	Holland				
Points					

What to do
Explain that the children have to find a word beginning with the letters across the top for each of the categories down the side. You can add to the categories, making them more specific according to the ability of your class.

You can award points for each space filled. Extra points can be given for answers offered by only one pupil.

Stick it in

Age range
Three to seven.

Group size
Individuals.

What you need
Stiff card,
used matchsticks,
marking pen,
golf tees and
hole punch (optional).

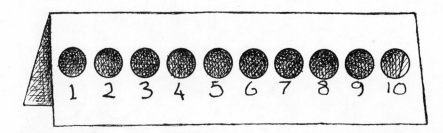

What to do
Prepare a number line as shown on a strip of stiff card. Mark in holes. The child can stick a matchstick into the right hole as required. Younger children may find it easier to use golf tees as pegs. If so, you will need to pre-punch holes in the card.

The child should insert the appropriate number of pegs into each number line, and order them from one through to ten. He or she could then be asked: 'Which number is the same as your age?'; 'Which number line has the most pegs?'; 'Which number line has more pegs than three but not as many as five?'

29

How many dog biscuits?

Age range
Three to six.

Group size
Individuals.

What you need
Tray with hollows
(eg baking tray or
polystyrene packing
from a box of apples),
pictures of dogs,
small dog biscuits,
container.

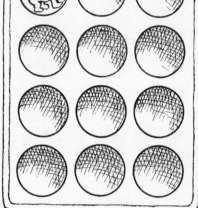

What to do
The dog pictures are placed in the hollows of the tray.
The child places an appropriate number of biscuits by
each dog, working from the teacher's directions, for
example: 'if each dog is to have three biscuits, how many
biscuits will you need altogether?'; 'how many dogs
could have five biscuits each?'; 'how many dogs get
more?'; 'how many dogs are there?'. Children can also
work on their own, sorting and counting.

    Note: Sometimes a child will try to eat the biscuits. Do
not encourage this!

Ice-cream numbers

Age range
Five to eight.

Group size
Individuals.

What you need
Pieces of card,
pen,
pieces of paper,
crayons,
container.

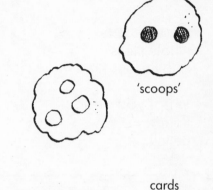

'scoops'

cards

 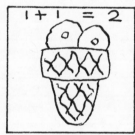 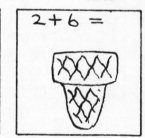

What to do
Draw out ice-cream cones on to cards. Lay them out on
the table. Also draw and colour in scoops of ice-cream
covered in varying numbers of chocolate chips, cherries
etc. Cut these out and place them in a container. The child
draws out the first scoop and places it on a cone. They
then draw out the second and place it on another cone.
They should record the combination as an addition sum,
on a piece of paper. An example might be as follows:
one cone has five chocolate chips and the other six
cherries. The sum should read: $5 + 6 = 11$

    The same principle can be applied to subtraction. You
can also try double scoops and triple scoops.

Word crocodiles

Age range
Seven to thirteen.

Group size
Whole class
or groups.

What you need
A dictionary per pair.

Follow-up
The words can be spelt. Points can be awarded for
beginning with the right letter, as well as for correct
spelling. In this way most children can gain points. Pupils
can also work in pairs, taking it in turns to say or write
down their words, whilst the other checks it in a
dictionary.

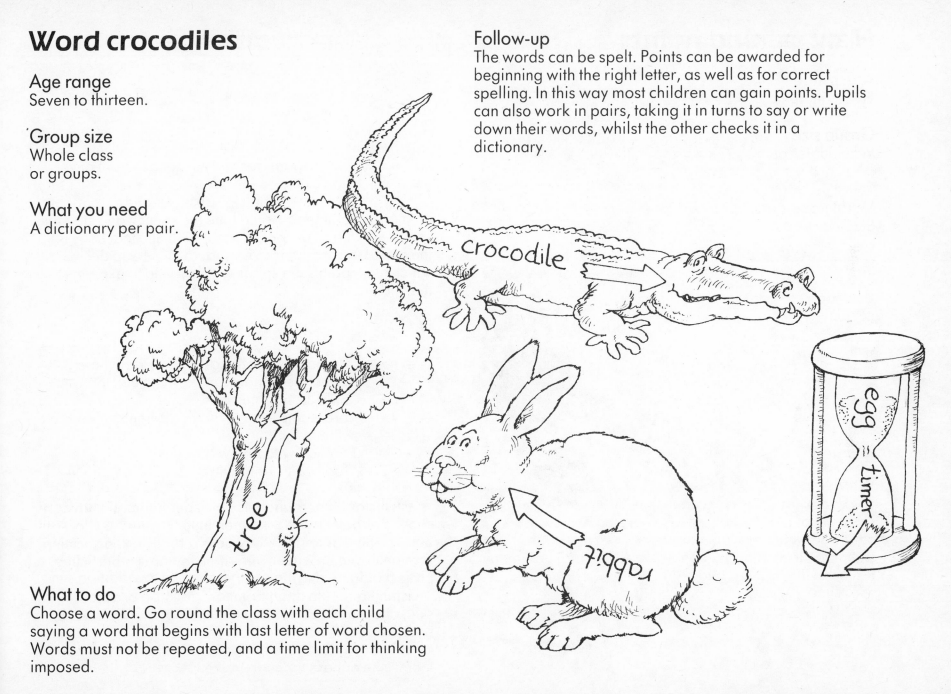

What to do
Choose a word. Go round the class with each child
saying a word that begins with last letter of word chosen.
Words must not be repeated, and a time limit for thinking
imposed.

Main talking points

Age range
Five to thirteen.

Group size
Whole class or
small groups.

What you need
Stop clock
or timer
(optional).

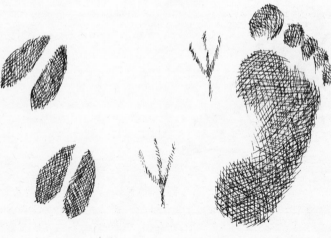

What to do
Ask volunteers to speak for thirty seconds about any topic which you or they might choose: for example 'feet', 'eyes', 'cats', 'noses', 'boats', 'cards', 'grandparents' etc.

Another volunteer should time the speech and stop the speaker at the appropriate point. With the teacher's help the rest of the group or class should then try to decide which main points the speaker was trying to explain to the audience:

Feet

⟶	Purposes – walking, kicking, running etc
⟶	Structure – shape, make-up, heel, toes etc
	Skin, bones, muscles etc
⟶	problems – corns, bunions, hammer-toes etc
⟶	smelly feet!
	objects with and without feet
⟶	footprints, animal tracks

Ask the audience what else the speaker might have spoken about if there had been time. Produce a chart as above. This part of the exercise is a really brainstorming session. It can provide orientation towards a particular project or item of topic work.

Listening for the main point of a talk is a practical study skill, and a most useful skill to develop. Children will be encouraged to listen more carefully to what the teacher says. They will be more likely to ask what was the main 'point' she or he is trying to make.

Sequencing skills

Age range
Five to seven.

Group size
Pairs.

What you need
Copy page 106
or copies of other verse,
scissors,
envelopes.

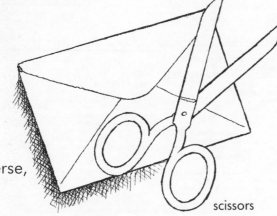
scissors

Humpty Dumpty sat on the wall, ...

snippets

All the king's horses and all the king's men, ...

What to do
Each pair is given a copy of one nursery rhyme or one
poem, a pair of scissors and an envelope. The pairs first
read the nursery rhymes together, and then cut them into
sentence strips as shown. When all are cut they should be
jumbled up and put in the envelope. Each of the pair then
draws out a strip in turn and tries to assemble them in the
correct sequence, 'putting the poem together again'. This
gives practice in both reading and study skills and in the
sequencing of ideas when writing. If there is any time left,
the completed version can be copied down. Later, it
might be illustrated for a class book on nursery rhymes or
verse.

Dictionary skills

Age range
Seven to thirteen
(or younger able pupils).

Group size
Whole class, groups, or individuals.

What you need
One dictionary per person,
paper,
pencils.

What to do
The size of each group will depend on the number of
dictionaries available. Ask the pupils to close the books
firmly and stand the book up with the binding facing
away from them. They must then try to open the book
exactly at the mid-point. They should record the letter of
the alphabet where the book came open. They repeat this
carefully five times. It may well fall open at the same letter
each time. They repeat this to find the end of the first
quarter of the book and then the start of last quarter. The
book is then sectioned into the four quartiles, for
example, A–E, F–N, O–T, U–Z. This sectioning makes it
easy to find a word in only three or four moves.

There will of course be slight variations in the quartiles,
depending on the different dictionaries used. Ask the
pupils to make up a mnemonic to help them remember
their quartiles, such as 'apples, elephants, nuts and
sausages' for 'AENS'.

33

Scanning exercises

Age range
Seven to thirteen.

Group size
Whole class or pairs.

What you need
Old telephone directories,
stop clock or timer.

```
NATIONAL TYRE SERVICE Ltd—
   Leamington Spa, 16 Court St ............. Leamington Spa 22228
   Do.................................................. Leamington Spa 22369
   Coventry, 67 Gosford St ........................... Coventry 26414
      70 Spon End ...................................... Coventry 74206
   Nuneaton, Freer St,Attleborough ................. Nuneaton 382260
   Service Divisional Office,
      Coventry, 70 Spon End ........................... Coventry 713303
   Stratford-upon-Avon, Masons Rd ........ Stratford-on-A 205285
National Union of Mine Workers,
                    17 Bulkington Rd..Bedworth 313181
National Union of Sheet Metal Workers & Coppersmiths,
                    26 Coundon Rd..Coventry 22920
NATIONAL UTILITY SERVICES Ltd—
   Energy & Telecoms Cost Control Analysts,
      Carolyn Ho, Dingwall Rd,Croydon ................01-681 2500
National Vacuum Cleaner Services (Coventry),
                    304 Holbrook La..Coventry 689087
National Vegetable Research Station—
   Wellesbourne...................................... Stratford-on-A 840382
   Caretaker, (After 5.00 p.m.)..................... Stratford-on-A 841756
   Glasshouse Supt, (After 5.00 p.m.)......... Stratford-on-A 840506
   Sports & Social Club .......................... Stratford-on-A 840559
National Videovan Rugby, Home Video Hire,
                    80/82 Railway Ter..Rugby 70817
National Vulcan Engineering Insurance Group Ltd, District
   Bank Chambers,Bennetts Hl,Birmingham..021-643 7607
NATIONAL WESTMINSTER BANK PLC—
   Agric Office ......................................... Coventry 553721
   Area Office,
      Coventry Area Off,Copthall Ho,Eaton Rd ....... Coventry 553131
      24 Hour Card Loss Centre .............................01-588 3600
   Branches,
      Balsall Common & Berkswell,
         299 Kenilworth Rd...................... Berkswell 32172
         Do............................................... Berkswell 32811
      Bedworth,
         12 King St ................................... Bedworth 319016
      Coventry,
```

```
   Cranmore, Birmingham Rd,Kings Coughton..Alcester 763445
Nayee A, 32 York St.................................... Rugby 61278
Nayee H.R, 42 York St................................. Rugby 62265
Nayee R.R, 61 Avenue Rd ............................ Rugby 76765
Nayee Somabhai, 27 Bridget St...................... Rugby 78991
Nayer Haines Ltd, 1/7 Bright St.................... Coventry 663626
Nayer-Haines Ltd, Roofing Contrs—
   155a St. Georges Rd............................. Coventry 552292
   Mill Cott,Common La,Corley ................. Fillongley 41274
Nayler W.E, 27 Stratford Rd........................ Warwick 495718
Nayler A, 6 Louisa Ward Clo........................ Marton 633229
NAYLOR A.J,Bldr & Contr, 36 Nightingale La .... Coventry 73646
Naylor A.J, Jnr, 43 Styvechale Av................. Coventry 76972
Naylor A.M, 26 Shorncliffe Rd ..................... Keresley 4147
Naylor A.M, 89 Upr Spon St......................... Coventry 58179
Naylor A.M.T, Moreton Ho Cott, Moreton Morrell,
         Moreton Morrell..Leamington Spa 651760
Naylor A.P, 13 Bridgetown Rd........... Stratford-on-A 294364
Naylor B.D, 172 Yewdale Cres...................... Coventry 614959
Naylor C, 5 Fraser Clo........................... Chapel End 394793
Naylor C.C, 14 Blandford Dv....................... Coventry 610875
Naylor D, 21 Dalton Rd............................. Bedworth 313997
Naylor D, 46 Latham Rd............................ Coventry 714490
Naylor D.G, 93 Baker Av................... Stratford-on-A 69244
Naylor E, 6 Livingstone Av, Long Lawford................Rugby 2923
Naylor E, 54 Merlin Av,Nuneaton ............... Chapel End 396995
Naylor Fred, 304 Kenilworth Rd,Balsall Com ....... Berkswell 34246
Naylor F, 44 Lincroft Cres........................ Coventry 713196
```

What to do
If you wish to carry out this activity as an exercise for the whole class, hand out copies of the same page of the directory. The teacher's copy should have five names underlined. When everyone is listening carefully, read out one of the underlined names at random, say 'Naylor, PB!'. They must try to find his name as fast as they can and tell you the right telephone number. Record the fastest times on the board. Be sure to make a note of those who can read but are very slow at this activity.

Have two practice runs. Before the third turn discuss the strategies they might use, such as scanning bottom and top names in each column to locate the key one, and then sectioning the column. Do they start at the top of the first column, and work slowly down? Is this the most efficient strategy?

Give two further trials to see if they have speeded up at all.

If working in pairs, give each pair a different page of the directory. Each one of the pair should take it in turns to select at random two names and telephone numbers from their page. Give an example or they may miss out the initials and number. The second of the pair should test the first, and then vice versa. If they all start together, the teacher can still record the time for them. After a couple of trials, the teacher should discuss strategies as before. They should then select two more names and repeat the exercise.

Practise with this from time to time. It is a useful study skills exercise. The pupils will think more about the way in which they perform skills and learn tasks. These kinds of activities will help them learn independently at a later stage.

Kim's game

Age range
Three to thirteen.

Group size
Whole class or
small group.

What you need
Tray,
cover,
collection of small objects.

What to do
This game is named after Rudyard Kipling's young hero, Kim.

Place a number of objects on the tray and cover them. Put the tray where everyone can see it. Tell them they will have some time to look at the things on it, and that then you will take it away. They will have to remember what was on the tray. The number of objects and the time given to look at them will depend on the age and ability of the class. You might take away or add an item, and show them the tray again.

You can tell them how many things were there or not.

You can ask them to tell you, or write down as much as they can remember. Explain that this game is an exercise to improve their powers of observation and to make them better at paying attention.

Follow-up
If the children write a list, you can make the game into a competition. Stop everyone when the first one has finished, or the first three or five, depending on how many are playing. Next time, the class can prepare their own trays and try them out on each other.

A discussion of the different ways of remembering is usually very helpful and interesting. Make a class record of these strategies. One day they may be useful:

- clustering things together in similar groups or like telephone numbers, eg 01-549 1411;
- repeating them under the breath (rehearsal);
- trying to imagine the position of the objects placed on the tray;
- imagining them with extra features eg watch's face.

35

Listening Kim

Age range
Seven to thirteen.

Group size
Small groups
or individuals.

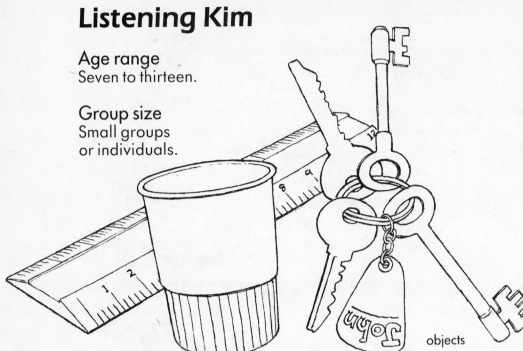

objects

What you need
Small, unbreakable objects which, when dropped, make
a recognisable sound – full match box, pencil, ruler, keys,
plastic cup etc; paper; pencils.

What to do
Sit the group in a circle and show them the articles. You
can explain what you are going to do, and practise by
asking them to close their eyes and then listen when you
drop an article. Then they turn facing outwards in a
circle. No cheating is allowed! You drop the articles, on
the floor or on a tray. You can ask them to draw, write
down or tell you what they think you've dropped. This
could be set up behind a screen (two tables with some
card between them) – it is difficult for children not to
peep!

Association Kim

Age range
Seven to thirteen.

Group size
Whole class or
small groups.

What you need
Objects as for Kim's game.

What to do
The group sits in a circle, looking at the tray of prepared
objects. You then mention an object associated with those
on the tray: for example, you might say 'blackboard' for
chalk, or 'hair' for a comb. The group has to say, write
down or draw what they think is linked to the word you
have said.
   The game can be varied by using abstract ideas. For
scissors you might say 'cut'; for a 'pin' you could say
'fasten'.

Butchers and bakers

Age range
Seven to thirteen.

Group size
Whole class,
groups,
or individuals.

What you need
Paper,
pencils.

What to do
Note spelling errors which appear in the pupil's work. If suffixes such as '-er' or '-cian' prove to be a problem, arrange a brief teach-in on them.

Explain that many base words have '-er' added to them when they refer to the jobs that people do. To each verb or 'doing' word '-er' is added to make it into 'the person who does . . .' – for example, teach-er, build-er, farm-er, make-r, play-er. They should then complete some others: weld-, swim-, strike-, hit-, sweep-. Now ask the pupils to make up ten examples of their own. Sometimes there is already an 'e' on the verb and so only 'r' is added, eg strike-r, make-r.

Explain that '-or' or '-cian' as suffixes also mean 'the one who'. There are fewer of them to watch out for. Make a list such as the following by questioning and then recording: doctor, sailor, professor etc.; magician, electrician, statistician, mathematician etc. The pupils should add to their list as they find new words.

Diagrams

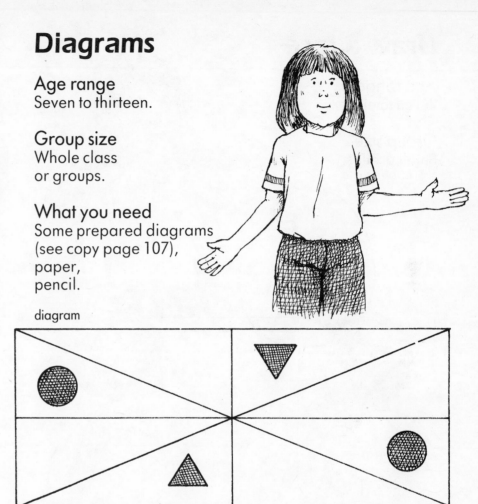

Age range
Seven to thirteen.

Group size
Whole class
or groups.

What you need
Some prepared diagrams
(see copy page 107),
paper,
pencil.

diagram

What to do
One child comes to you and is shown a diagram, without the class being able to see it. He or she then describes the diagram, and the class attempts to draw the diagram from the description. The diagrams are held up and the level of accuracy noted. The results can often be very funny. This procedure can be repeated. It can be developed by children producing their own diagrams and testing them.

Draw a face

Age range
Seven to eleven.

Group size
Small groups.

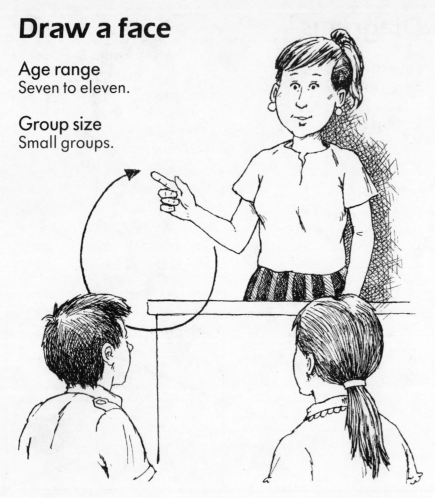

What to do
Ask the group to watch carefully while you draw
something in the air. With your index finger, draw a face.
First draw the outline clockwise. Then the right eye, then
the left eye, nose downward, mouth right to left.

   Ask someone to draw exactly what you have drawn.
Those who don't manage it must watch again. Those who
do must not explain. It will take some children quite some
time to realise that you are drawing a face.

Anagrams

Age range
Seven to thirteen.

Group size
Groups or
individuals.

What you need
Chalk,
paper,
pencil,
cards.

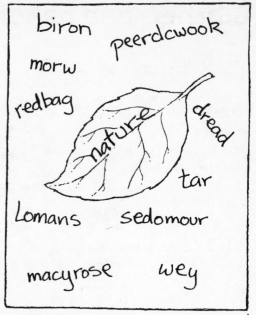

card

What to do
Prepare some anagrams and write them out on cards or
on the blackboard. At the beginning, keep to a chosen
theme. Show the anagrams, and ask the children to put
them right. You might give them a clue. When several
examples have been completed, suggest some new
themes, or ask for suggestions. Children may then make
their own anagrams, and pass them round for
reassembling correctly.

   See copy page 108 for sets of useful topic-related
anagrams (with answers).

Follow-up
Anagrams related to a topic can be written randomly on
a card, with the topic word in the middle. A picture can
then be drawn on the back. The best can go in a class
puzzle book, or on display.

Link's cube

Age range
Seven to thirteen.

Group size
Whole class
or group of any size.

What you need
Pencil,
paper,
or blackboard and chalk,
27 toy bricks
and green stickers
(optional).

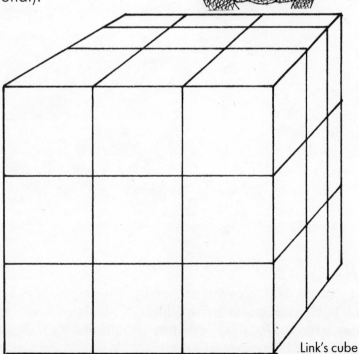

Link's cube

What to do
Check that the children know what a cube is. Ask the children to close their eyes and imagine that they can see a large, bright green cube. In their minds they are to see if they can turn the cube round and look at the back, front and underneath. They should then open their eyes. Ask who was able to do this. Next they should close their eyes again, and conjure up the cube. Now explain that someone has cut their cube up into 27 tiny pieces, all cubes. Where it has been cut, all the *inside* faces are yellow. Look inside the cube. Ask how many of the 27 little cubes have:

3 green sides (8)
2 green sides (12)
1 green side (6)
No green sides (1)

   Many will be puzzled, and will only get a little way with this. A few will begin to work it out correctly and get some of the answers. One or two will answer correctly. After they have tried to imagine the answers and counted them in their mind's eye, allow them to draw the diagram on paper or on the blackboard. They may help each other discover that there are three rows of nine cubes. Let them try to work out the answers from the drawings.

Follow-up
Those who are still puzzled should, in another spare five minutes, check up on the cube. They can count the answers in three dimensions. Borrow 27 toy bricks (cubes) and let them stick on green dots to mark the outside faces. They can then be assembled and counted. The group could also make their own cube out of clay/Plasticine.

Brahma tower

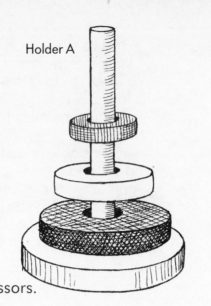

Holder A

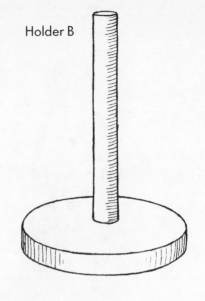

Holder B

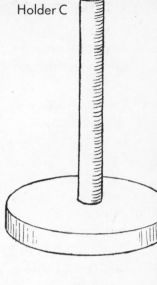

Holder C

Age range
Seven to thirteen.

Group size
Whole class,
groups or
individuals.

What you need
Coloured rings and pegs,
or blackboard and coloured chalks,
or cardboard, coloured pens and scissors.

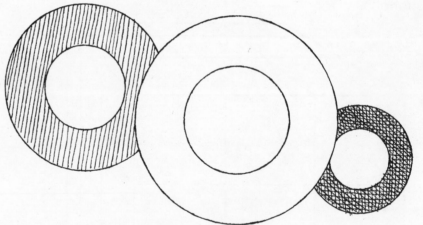

What to do
This is another opportunity for some mental gymnastics!
Holder (a) has on it three coloured rings (say, red, green
and blue). They are in decreasing order of size. These
rings have all to be transferred to either holder (b) or (c) –
but the following rules must be obeyed:
- only one ring can be moved at a time.
- only smaller rings can be put on top of larger ones.
What is the least number of moves that this will take?
(*Answer*: seven).

The children should try to solve this problem mentally.
Note the children carefully who can do problems such as
this or Link's cube. Both problems demand the kind of
skills which help in engineering design. Are these the
engineers of the future?

The problem can also be done on the blackboard with
coloured chalks, using pencil and paper, or using home-
made rings of coloured cardboard.

Follow-up
Individuals or pairs who are more able or practised can
try a variant as a five-minute filler. Give them four rings to
move from (a) to (b) or (c). They should first try it mentally,
and then put it to the test. (*Answer*: 15).

Snowmen

Age range
Five to seven.

Group size
Individuals.

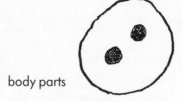

body parts

What you need
Card,
felt-tip pen,
pencil,
pieces of paper,
containers.

adding cards

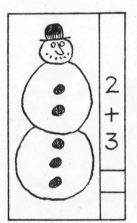
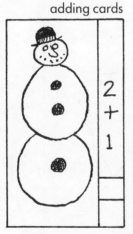
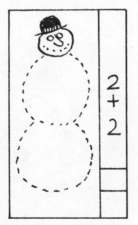

What to do
Cut large and small circles from the card to make the parts of snowmen. The body should be in two sections, each with a different number of buttons. Arrange the snowmen parts in various patterns. The child must write down the combinations as addition sums. For example, two buttons and three buttons: $2 + 3 = 5$.

Sort and post

Age range
Three to seven.

Group size
Individuals.

What you need
Pictures of clothes and materials showing various patterns and types, card,
sorting box,
container for pattern cards,
glue,
scissors.

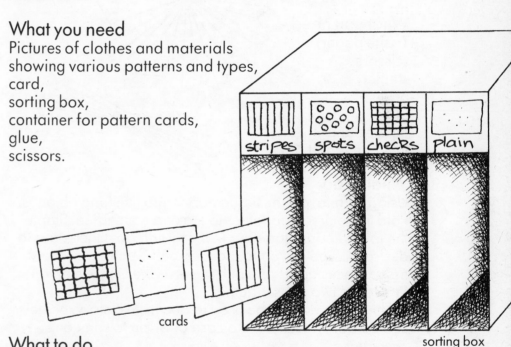

cards

sorting box

What to do
Collect together magazine pictures of clothes and scraps of material. Glue them on to cards, and place them in a box for sorting.

Children should find as many ways to sort the cards as possible, and then discuss why they have sorted in the way they did. Children may enjoy carrying out a survey of the class, to see how many children are wearing each of these patterns. A simple graph may be made of how many different materials children are wearing.

Paper flowers

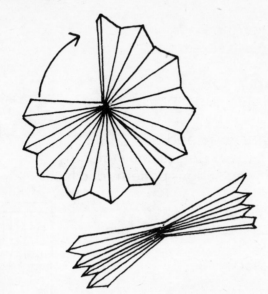

Age range
Seven to ten.

Group size
Individuals.

What you need
Tissue paper,
scissors,
stapler,
paste,
glitter,
pipe cleaner,
tulle (optional).

What to do
Using a knife, cut the tissue paper into five long oblongs.
Fold these pieces together to make a concertina. Staple
the folded paper together in the middle. Cut the edges to
desired shape eg round, pointed etc. Gently ease the
tissue pieces apart and pull towards the centre staple.
Staple the two joins together.

These flowers can be used to decorate a story, or they
can be worn, stuck on to a card or given to someone
special.

To make the flowers seasonal, yellow and green may
be used for spring; for winter use red and white. Make a
saucer of paste and have a saucer of glitter. Dip the
flower in the glue and then in the glitter. This will give a
'frosty' effect. To put a stem on, bend a pipe cleaner
around the middle of the flower after putting the staple in.
Instead of using just tissue paper, you might try making
every other sheet a piece of tulle. This material can look
very effective.

One-fold fun

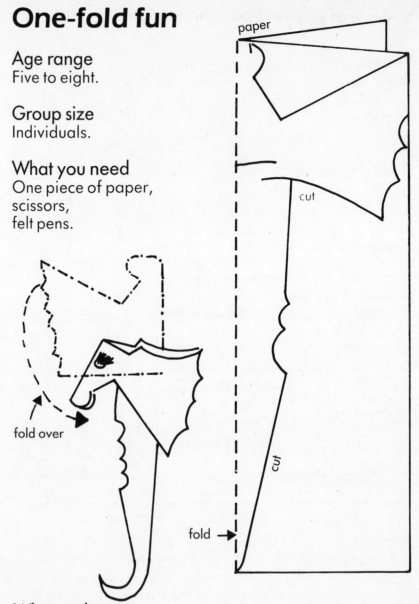

Age range
Five to eight.

Group size
Individuals.

What you need
One piece of paper,
scissors,
felt pens.

What to do
Fold a piece of paper in half. Draw the shape required
and cut out.

Fold the sea – horse's head where indicated which helps to give a 3D effect. Curl tail round a pencil to give a turned up effect.

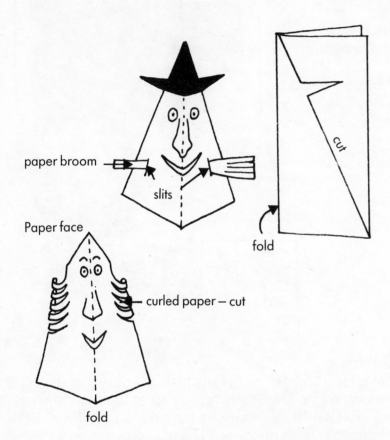

Cut a paper broom and slot the handle through the two slits.

To alter the shape of the face, cut oblong, round, square and triangular shapes. To make paper curls, simply cut the edge of the paper into strips and bend.

Counters

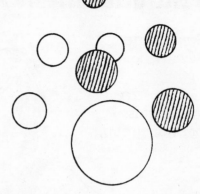

Age range
Seven to thirteen.

Group size
Whole class,
pairs,
individuals.

What you need
Large number of coloured counters (at least ten per child, and at least five of a different colour). Pencil and paper for recording if wished.

What to do
Ask children to lay out five counters of one colour and then five of another colour, thus:

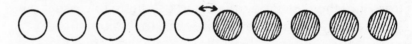

What are the minimum number of moves to make all ten counters alternate in colour? They can only change the positions of counters next to each other.

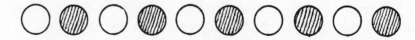

Firstly they should try to do it in their heads, and then they should check, working it through with the counters. This can be extended into a whole lesson. The children can record their moves on a chart, starting with one pair. They should look at the pattern of results on the chart. How many moves would it take, for example, to get 20 counters into alternating rows?

Test your memory

Age range
Seven to ten.

Group size
Whole class
or small group.

What to do
Tell the children you are going to test their memory.
Stress that they must be quiet, and ask them to close their
eyes. When you say a letter, they are to think of three
words beginning with that letter. When they have thought
of them, they must open their eyes, but not say anything or
disturb those still thinking. This is a good way of calming
a group of children, and you can learn from watching
their reactions.

When several children have opened their eyes, stop the
others and say: 'All open your eyes. Let's see who can
remember their three words'. Ask one of those children
who opened their eyes first. Check a few more, and if
they find these words easy then move on to five. Some
children find this exercise difficult and need several
attempts and encouragement before they can think of
their words. Others can barely wait to tell you their
words. With a bright group, you can move on to more
words or ask for words of more than one syllable.

Words within words

Age range
Six to thirteen.

Group size
Any number.

What you need
Paper,
pencil.

What to do
Write a long word or name on the blackboard such as
Constantinople. Give them four minutes to write down as
many words as they can make from the original word. Put
the longest lists up on the wall as a display.

Other words you might try include: maintenance,
instrumentation, experimentation, interrogation,
disturbance, penitentiary, parsimonious, ambulatory,
salvationist.

Any important new words which are being read in
stories or are otherwise topical can be used for this filler.
It will also encourage word analysis and synthesis skills.

Egg boxes

Age range
Five to seven.

Group size
Small groups of two or three.

What you need
Egg boxes,
small ball
or counters,
paper,
pencil.

What to do

Write a number in each cup of the egg box, or else put in pieces of paper with numbers written on them. The children throw the ball or counter into the cup and add up their total (they might have two goes each or more). They can write down each others' score, and compare results.

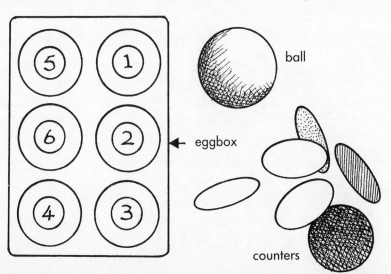

ball

eggbox

counters

To make the game more challenging you can write on the counters:

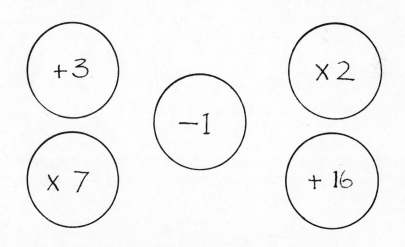

In this way the value of numbers in the cups can be increased, or decimals and fractions introduced.

Instant lessons

Memory checks

3-7-4-0-2-1

Age range
Six to thirteen.

Group size
Whole class.

What you need
Paper,
pencils.

What to do
Give out paper and pencils. Ask the pupils to listen very carefully. Explain you are going to measure how good their memories are at the moment.

Read out the following sets of digits in a monotonous voice, at a regular spacing of about one digit per second.

Ask the pupils to listen to the *whole* list, and then try to write it down. Read out the list again so that they can check their answers.

Note: for 1–9–2 pupils should record 1–9–2. Point out that 129 is not correct: the numbers have to be in the correct position too.

Give one mark for each digit in the correct place. Read out the lists:

1	9	2				Possible	3
3	1	8				Score	3
9	6	7	0				4
2	5	4	8				4
7	5	1	3	9			5
6	0	2	7	3			5
3	7	4	0	2	1		6
4	0	1	6	7	2		6

Which was their best score? Pupils at about the six-year-old level should have spans of four to five digits. By the age of ten the average pupil achieves a span of six. Adults have a memory span of between five and nine digits, with a mean of seven.

Some very able pupils may have spans of nine or ten digits or even more at quite a young age. If the pupils' span is poor, it may be that listening skills need to be developed. It could be that anxiety over numbers causes confusion and makes them forget. Some children develop and learn more slowly, and their scores may be not quite as good as the others. You might try the memory check again at the end of the year to see how the pupils are progressing, so it is important to record their best scores and their totals.

The pupils' actual scores can be used to show how to record scores and make histograms, as well as for discussion:

```
O  3   x x x x
   4   x x x x
   5   x x x x  x x x x
O  6   x x x x  x x
```

or

```
O  3   ++++  ++++
   4   ++++  ++++  ||||
   5   ++++  ++++  ++++  ++++
O  6   ++++  ++++
```

Design a logo

Age range
Six to thirteen.

Group size
Whole class, groups or individuals.

What you need
Copy page 109, coloured pencils or paints.

What to do
This can be a starter lesson prior to outdoor activities on transport. Alternatively, it could be substituted for an outdoor lesson which is rained off. Discuss with the children the advertisements they have seen on the side of lorries. These may explain what the lorry is carrying. For example, a truck may be painted to look like the chocolate bars it carries, so that it looks like a huge chocolate box. Explain how trucking and truckers with their CB helped to popularise the image of lorry drivers and about the search for a strong trucking-like name for the chocolate bar.

Companies often create a symbol, or 'logo', which suggests their company instead of using their names on the sides of the lorries. Examples might be:

Ask if the group can think of any logos which they have seen and discuss them. Try to help them think of why they are used rather than the whole names. Possible reasons might be succinctness, memorability, visual interest, etc.

Explain that each child should now choose a product for which they are the 'company designer'. They must then try to design a 'logo' or an interesting advertisement for the product to fit into the side of the lorry (see copy page 109). Their designs should be accompanied by a brief description of the product. This may be written, or verbal if with younger children. The product itself could be a real one (the logo could be sent off to the company for their consideration), or it could be an imaginary one.

After working on their designs, each child should start compiling a notebook keeping a record of which advertisements they have seen on lorries, noting especially the clever and interesting ones. This can be an activity which passes the time helpfully during boring car journeys.

Follow-up
Make a badge 'logo': many teachers' centres have badge-making machines which you can borrow. They are also fairly cheap to buy, and can be useful for fund-raising events.

Talk about non-commercial uses of logos. Does the local council use one? Is the school badge a sort of logo? Why do schools have badges? You might talk about symbols of religions: a Christian cross, an Islamic crescent, a Buddhist wheel, for example.

Is there something wrong?

Age range
Seven to thirteen.

Group size
Whole class,
groups or
individuals.

What you need
Copy page 110,
pencils,
paper,
scissors,
paste or stapler,
mounting paper.

What to do
Take copies of page 110. There should be at least one
between two pupils. Read the story to the class and let
them follow it on their copy. Ask them whether they think
this is a good story, or whether they think there is
something wrong with it.

They should tell you that the story has a beginning but
no middle or end. Its good points are that it sets a scene
and builds up some interest in an event. However, instead
of working through to this event, it ignores it completely.

It continues setting the scene and simply tells the reader
about the context. This is often the way a writer builds up
tension in the reader of the story, but this one fails to
develop the story further.

The pupils should then discuss in pairs possible
implications of the plot. For example, what might the
metal object have been? What would she decide to do
about it on the way to work? Let them do this for just a
few minutes. Give no help. Stop the pairs and feed in
further information. Discuss the following, looking for
other clues present in the text which might help: probably
no husband, family or pets; probably lives in a flat (goes
through to kitchen and *down* to car); today was a special
day; was the metal object connected with that day, or
not? She was not diet conscious; she spent at least an
hour over breakfast and getting ready for work; she
owned a car and went to work in it.

Would the story be easier to complete if we know what
she had received? Would it be more interesting if just one
or two crucial details were changed? Each group could
be allowed to change one detail if necessary.

Let the pairs of pupils discuss what they think should
happen at the two critical points in the story. When they
have decided and agreed a good insert, they should cut
the printed sheet at their critical points and write in the
pieces which they have agreed. The final version should
be pasted (or stapled) together on another sheet or
sheets of paper.

A sample of the stories should be read aloud to the rest
of the class. At the end of the lesson all the finished
versions should be mounted and set at eye level on the
walls round the class, so that everyone can read what the
others have written. Later, a discussion can ensue on the
best features of some of the stories. Discuss the ways in
which pupils have created different metal objects for the
heroine to find.

Coat stories

Age range
Seven to thirteen.

Group size
Whole class,
or small groups.

What you need
Dirty, ragged old overcoat,
launderette bag
or newspaper and string,
brown envelope,
crust of bread,
small padlock key,
assorted objects.

What to do
Carry an old overcoat into the class, concealed in a bag
or wrapped up as a parcel with newspaper and string.
Gather the pupils round you, either on the carpet as for a
story, or sitting and standing closer to the teaching area.
Explain that you found something lying at the back of
your garden shed or garage. It wasn't yours, you just
found it there yesterday; you have brought it to show to
them. Can they guess what the bag contains? When the
coat is revealed, ask different pupils to describe what
they can actually see. How many different features has it?
Could these be clues as to who its owner might be? What
sort of person could that be – a gardener, a tramp? How
might they discover further clues? Look for a name-tag, a
maker's label. Look in the pockets:– 'discover' a brown
envelope, with a piece of bread in it; 'discover' a key, or
any other objects of interest. Dare to put the coat on.

Imagine what the person might look like, how tall; where
was he or she going, and what might be the significance
of the things in the pockets? When the pupils'
imaginations are suitably fired, send them back to their
places to record the clues. They can then work out a story
about the owner of the old coat. Read out the stories and
bind them into a class book.

Follow-up 1
What is an editor? What makes a good story? Make
copies of two of the best detective stories. Let pairs of
pupils select one of the stories to work on together. Their
job is to be editors for a short story book. They have to
improve the story, by working on the details given. They
should 'fill out' the characters with more description and
detail; improve or add to the chain of events described;
provide more 'atmosphere'.

Compare what the various editors have done with their
basic story outlines. Editors can, if they prefer, work on
their own stories but encourage them still to work in pairs
so that they can discuss their thoughts and spark off
further ideas.

Follow-up 2

This can be a follow-up or an alternative activity. Present the coat as before. This time, when the pupils have described it and discussed what the pockets contained, ask them to reflect not just upon the owner but upon the coat itself. What is its history; what was it like when it was a young, 'smarter' coat; who did it belong to then; how did it pass from hand to hand, and come to its present state? What life, or lives, has this coat seen? What would happen if it were a magic coat? Suppose when you put it on, you looked out from it through the eyes of one of its previous owners? Let one of the pupils try this, with eyes closed. Where would they be in time, and what would they be able to see? How long is the life of a coat? Can it last a hundred years? Have they seen old coats and uniforms in museums? Next time they must make a careful note of the age of any clothes they see in museums, and think about what those clothes might have seen.

MAN 1660

MAN 1740

WOMAN 1920

Lost and found

Age range
Seven to thirteen.

Group size
Whole class, or small groups.

What you need
Copies of 'lost and found' and 'for sale' columns from the local newspaper.

What to do
Ask the pupils to think of something that they have treasured, which they have lost at some time. Discuss their various experiences and how they felt. What did they do to try to recover their lost item? Make a list on the blackboard of what actions they could take if they lost something. For example:

- ask someone else to search with you in case you have overlooked it.
- ask other people if they recall seeing it.
- place an annoucement in a local shop window, for a small fee, or at the school gate.
- advertise in the local newspaper, for a larger fee.
- a reward might be offered.

Ask the pupils to write a full description of what it is they have lost, without putting a title to it. Read these aloud. Find out if others in the class can recognise what it is and suggest where it might be found. Next, ask each pupil to compose an advertisement for the newspaper, to try to recover their lost belongings. They have, however, only £1 to spend and each word costs 10p. They must therefore now condense their description into ten words. Give out examples of lost and found columns in the local newspapers, so that they can compare their efforts with those from real life.

The travelling shoe

Age range
Six to thirteen.

Group size
Whole class
or small groups.

What you need
One well-worn shoe.

What to do
Explain to the pupils that on the way to school you found
this shoe lying in the road. It looks a much-loved and
well-worn shoe, a much travelled shoe; it was obviously
on its way somewhere when it was lost. Who do they think
such a shoe might belong to? What would the person do
when he or she found they had lost one of their favourite
shoes? Now the travelling shoe is on its own, it only has
its memories, and nowhere new to go. If they could hear
it, what stories might it tell about where it had been and
the adventures it had had? Would it be fond of foreign
travel? Had it been to the Costa Brava, and seen a
bullfight? Tell the pupils to think about that shoe and its
owner and tell the story of one of its journeys. Older
pupils might think about whether it will be a shoe from
some region of the British Isles, with a local accent.
Perhaps it was made instead in Italy or Taiwan. Would it
understand its owner or the strange English customs?

'What is it?'

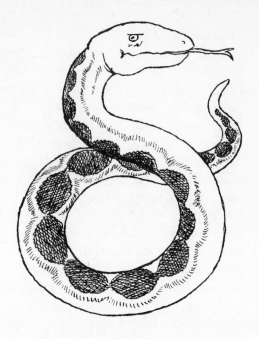

Age range
Six to eight.

Group size
Whole class
or small groups.

What you need
Writing paper,
pens or pencils.

What to do
Write up seven questions on the blackboard before the
lesson. Explain to the class that they have to work out
what the answers to the questions are. An example might
be as follows:

> **The Snake**
> What colour am I? (I am green and cool.)
> What shape am I? (I am long and thin.)
> What size am I? (I am small.)
> What noise do I make? (I hiss—sss at you.)
> How do I move?
> What do I eat?
> What am I?

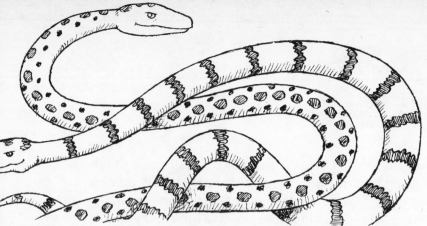

The pupils have to write the title *The Snake* in their books or on their papers, and then answer each of the questions, using a full sentence. Start off by giving them an example, using the class's answers to sample questions, as above. Ask them to complete the rest themselves or, if they wish, start from the beginning again. The various answers can be read out around the class. Praise those who have expressed snake-like features in the words they have chosen. Discuss onomatopoeia, if appropriate for the stage the pupils have reached. If not, refer to it in more everyday terms: 'hissing', 'slithering', 'green' and 'cool'. Explain that they have created a kind of poem and that not all poems rhyme. Later, you might read them some examples. Next, ask each member of the group to think of an animal for themselves. They should ask themselves the same kind of questions, but about the animal of their choice.

Get them to write. When several have finished they can read out their poems. The others must guess what they have written about. Pupils who write and think quickly will be able to do several of these 'poems' in a session. Slower pupils should be encouraged to complete at least one.

Their efforts can either be put into one large class book for them to read at will, or they can be mounted on cut-out animal shapes for display.

Survival kits

Age range
Six to thirteen.

Group size
Whole class, small groups or individuals.

What you need
Large matchboxes, old tobacco tins, enamel paint or coloured stickers.

What to do
The children should collect old tobacco tins, large matchboxes or other pocket-sized containers. They should decorate them with paint or coloured stickers. On the lids they should write:

SURVIVAL KIT

They should then make a list of the items they would put inside their box if they were stranded on a desert island. Each one must be essential for survival, and small enough to fit in the box. They should write down why they have included each item.

Follow-up
Over a period of time the pupils can collect together the actual items for their kits. They should keep their choices secret, but tell the teacher how they are getting on. Finally, there could be an exhibition of all the kits. The items could be discussed, and the lists displayed. Some time could be spent producing a composite kit for the whole class.

53

Class poems

Age range
Six to thirteen.

Group size
Whole class
or small groups.

What you need
Blackboard,
chalk,
paper,
pens,
pencils.

What to do
Before the class arrives, write a sentence on the board
such as:

The highwayman rode over the hill

Explain that together they are going to construct a
group poem and look at the ways in which writers
achieve their aims. Ask the children to say the first line
aloud, together but quietly. They should then pause and
think, to let their minds work on it. Then, at your signal,
repeat the first line aloud. Take down each of the lines
suggested, and ask the others to try these lines out by
repeating the first line and the new ones in turn. Reject
any which 'do not fit'. Do not rub them off yet, just put a
line through them. Allow any of the lines given to be
improved by inserting new words and crossing out old
ones, eg 'towards the far horizon' and 'saw the far
horizon'.

Even while discussions continue on one line, another
pupil may give you the third and fourth lines. Move on to
test these and then ask the class to remember the four
lines so far. Discuss improvements and alternatives.
Work slowly down through the poem. What will be
revealed with judicious questioning is that there is a
rhythm and meter established by the first line which can
be followed through and preserved in the rest of the
poem. In this instance it could match the galloping of a
horse. The meter can change when the horse's pace
changes.

You can also reveal to the pupils that although writers
work at many drafts of their writing, they seldom produce
a perfect copy at one go. This will emphasise the
importance of pupils re-reading their own work to re-
draft and improve it. It will teach them about writing for a
purpose.

The completed poem, when agreed, can be copied
down as handwriting practice and illustrated. To
reinforce the idea of movement and rhythm, read to them
one or two poems which illustrate this well, such as *John
Gilpin* by William Cowper.

Hypotheses

Age range
Four to eight.

Group size
Whole class, groups or individuals.

What you need
Shapes in preferably four colours (red, green, yellow and blue), sizes both large and small (*see copy page 111*). Make or collect a large and a small set of each colour.

Lego blocks serve very well, and add another variable, ie thickness/thinness. Thirty-two items and four variables make suitable problems to pose for older pupils. Pupils may cut out and colour in the shapes for you, and stick them to cardboard as prior activity.

What to do
Check first that the group know the colour and shape names, although this is not an essential prerequisite to the game. With the children's help, lay out the shapes so that they do not overlap. Ask the children to close their eyes.

When they all do, pick up at random one of the shapes and hide it in your hands or pockets so that they cannot see it.

In turn, the pupils round the group pick up their selection and show it to you and the others. The teacher says 'yes' if the colour they show is the same colour as the one in his or her other hand, or if the shape is the same. You do not tell them to which dimension you are saying 'yes'. You can say 'no' to those selections which do not represent either of the colours or shapes in your hand. When each pupil has selected a shape and you have responded, they then have to guess what the colour and shape is which you are holding. Everyone in the group is shown the card in your hand.

For young or less able children begin with only one attribute to guess, for example: 'What colour shape is the one in my hand?'. For older or more able children, begin with two attributes. You can then move up to three or four if you have blocks of different thicknesses.

Follow-up
When the pupils know how to play the game they can be divided into smaller groups. If you have enough items, the pupils can take turns in selecting and holding the problem shapes for others in the group to guess.

With three of four variables it is possible to play the game at a more complex level, by finding the least number of selections each person needs to make in order to solve the problem. Each group keeps a score sheet (*see copy page 112*).

Each individual takes turns in attempting to solve the problem. The others in the group pick up the shapes and show them. Discuss how the group can act to prevent an individual solving the problem. Explain that the group's task is to teach all its members to solve the problem in the fewest possible choices.

The elf's journey

Age range
Four to seven.

Group size
Whole class,
groups or
individuals.

What you need
Ball of clay about 8–10 cm in diameter for each child,
pencils and paper for older children who can write their
own stories, drawing paper and coloured pencils or
paint, scissors, copy page 113.

What to do
Ask the children how it would feel to be very, very tiny,
but still in their classroom. Discuss how *small* – about
15 cm, for example? Ask them about any stories which
they might have heard about 'little people'. What are
such people often called? What do they do? Show them
the picture from copy page 113. What would happen to
the children if they were to have a visit from an elf, and he
or she made a magic wish for them to become very tiny
too, just for one day in school? What would happen to
them? What would be the good things and what would be
the problems? Discuss their answers and suggestions,
and then say: 'Well now, let us find out!'. They are to
make a tiny little person just like the elf and take him or
her with them during the day to see what it would be like
to be so small.

The children then make their little people from the clay.
When they have finished, they can take them on a trip
round the classroom to see what they might find out.

When they have done this, they can return to their places
and draw and colour or paint a 'life-sized' picture of their
elf. Those who prefer can colour in the copy page
picture, but remind them that they will all look the same
and that elves, like people, probably look different.

As soon as they are all back in their places, ask them
what they have discovered so far.

They should continue drawing and painting until nearly
break-time. After packing up, discuss how the little
people might get out of the classroom, and so on.
Younger pupils will enjoy telling the rest of the class their
story, talking as though they are the little person.

At intervals throughout the day, review what has
happened to the little people. Music and movement work,
for example, could concentrate on small and light
movements. Pupils who can write should be encouraged
to write down their adventure as the small person.

Missing words

Age range
Six to thirteen.

Group size
Pairs.

What you need
One copy of the selected poem for each pupil. Two starter examples appear on copy page 114.

What to do
First delete key words from the poem before giving it out. For younger children, take out rhyming words so that it is easier for them to think of the word which is missing. For older children, take out key words which draw attention to the main ideas in the poem. Explain any other words which may prove to be stumbling blocks.

Working in pairs, the pupils have to try to complete the poem and so reconstruct the author's original meaning. Each pair discusses what the missing words might be, and then agree which to insert. After they have tried to do this, go over the missing words to let them know how many they have correct. Then read the whole poem aloud to them, or read it together. By working in pairs. One can promote discussion and extend speaking in sentences. It avoids the routine of closed questions from the teacher and one-word answers from the quicker children. You will be surprised by the pupils' greater interest, understanding and critical appreciation of the poem when worked through in this way. Sometimes pupils find more interesting words than the ones deleted. This makes for good discussion points and plenty of opportunity to praise constructive ideas.

Able pupils, when given a simple rhyming poem, enjoy the challenge of finding a replacement word which preserves the meaning but goes against the rhyme. Nursery rhymes are useful for this as practice items. Pupils become much more aware of the author's construction and the meanings of poems, when studying in this fashion. Simple comprehension activities, such as reading and discussing the meanings of words and phrases, cannot be of such help.

Deletion activities are often applied to prose, or given as cloze activities for reading comprehension tests.

A guinea-pig song
There was a little guinea-pig
Who, being little, was not ____.
He always walked upon his ____
And never tasted when he eat.

When from a place he run ____,
He never at the place did stay;
And while he run, as I am ____,
He ne'er stood ____ for young and old.
He often ____, was sometimes violent
And when he squeaked he ne'er was ____,
Though ne'er instructed by a ____,
He knew a ____ was not a rat.

One day, as I am certified,
He took a whim and fairly ____,
And as I am told by men of sense
He never has been living ____.

Anon
c1773

(Author's missing words: old, feet, away, told, still, squealed, silent, cat, mouse, died, since).

Design a machine

Age range
Seven to thirteen.

Group size
Whole class
or groups.

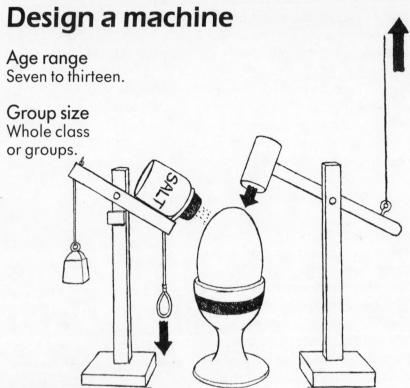

What you need
Pictures of Heath Robinson-type inventions (see copy page 115), paper and pencil.

What to do
Discuss the type of inventions specialised in by Heath Robinson. Collect a list of suggestions for class to develop for lazy people: pet–exerciser, room–tidier, homework robot, get–you–up–in–the–morning machine, egg–cracker, tooth or shoe cleaner . . . .

The class should then design inventions for themselves and name them 'The wonderful . . . machine'. Have a competition, for individuals or groups. Display them, and reward the most ingenious.

Captions and headlines

Age range
Seven to thirteen.

Group size
Small groups.

What you need
Magazine pictures, paper and pencil, scissors, glue, scrap paper, chalk.

THE GANG ARE RARIN' TO GO

Clowning about — nine-year-olds Emma Tovey, Sophie Parkinson, and Raphael Colledge.
© Heart of England Newspapers

What to do
Discuss a picture and its caption. Write some alternative captions on the board. Ask the children to write out some as well. Discuss which are most effective, and why. Children can choose their own picture and make up captions on scrap paper. When they have written a satisfactory one, the picture can be glued to paper and the caption written out neatly, above or below.

Display the finished work and vote for the best.

Follow-up 1
Arrange the class in groups of three. In an envelope, put a newspaper headline, an unrelated picture without a caption, and an unrelated story. The groups of three act as sub-editors, and have to invent appropriate captions for the picture, a story to go with the headline, and a headline to go with the story.

Follow-up 2
Study stories and captions from newspapers to see how they are constructed and why.

Following instructions 1

Age range
Six to eight.

Group size
Pairs.

What you need
String,
shoelaces,
neckties,
paper,
books,
ribbon.

What to do
The children should work in pairs, with one child telling the other what to do. No pointing is allowed (the instructors must sit on their hands). The other must do only what he or she is instructed to do in order to: fasten shoes, put on a tie, wrap up books, make a 'cat's cradle'.

Follow-up
You can develop this activity into giving and following written instructions for more complicated actions. One might have to write directions for one's partner to find his or her way to the office or hall. The other then has to follow them.

Following instructions 2

Age range
Eight to thirteen.

Group size
Pairs.

What you need
String and other materials, blindfolds.

What to do
In order to make a challenging verbal skills task with older groups, introduce blindfolds to the activity Following Instructions 1. Success is achieved when an example is completed with no interference from the seeing partner. The teacher can award ten points at the outset and knock off points every time there is an interference.

The purpose of this game is to encourage observation and precise communication skills. Note those pupils who are very good and those who are very poor. The latter will need guidance on how to explain things to someone else. This is an ability much needed in the world of work, in later years, and is a useful study skill whilst at school.

Shapes, forms and patterns

Age range
Three to five.

Group size
Small groups or
individuals.

What you need
Cut-out shapes
of two contrasting colours
(small, medium, large)
(see copy page 116),
containers for shapes,
glue,
glue brushes.

What to do
Decide which colours to use. If having a 'black and white'
week, choose those two colours and cut out lots of
shapes – small, medium and large – in each colour. Talk
to the children about making patterns using these shapes.
Try to encourage the children to continue their pattern
beyond the edge of the paper to see how long they can
make it. Encourage the children to discuss size, and to try
out their patterns before sticking them down. Children
can be very creative with patterns, and this activity is
excellent for discussing size, colour, and shape. You can
use a variety of base shapes as a background.

Touch messages

Age range
Eight to thirteen.

Group size
Groups or
individuals.

What you need
Tin foil paper,
Braille alphabet.

What to do
Ask the children to send some messages in Braille.
Carefully use a blunt pencil to press a dot on to the foil
paper.

Follow-up
Tell the story of Braille and its inventor. Read the story of
Helen Keller. Use other codes such as Morse to send
each other messages. Children will find a real blind
board fascinating, if you can obtain one.

A	B	C	D	E	F	G
H	I	J	K	L	M	N
O	P	Q	R	S	T	U	V
W	X	Y	Z			

What you need
Sheets of paper
(child-size),
chalk,
glue,
wool,
paint,
tissue paper,
fabric scraps,
silver paper,
cardboard for baskets,
hats, crowns, swords etc.

What to do
Use chalk to trace the outline of a child while he or she is lying on the large piece of paper. The outline can then be painted, decorated and filled in in various ways.

Each child can make the outline into a self-portrait or a group can work together to produce a paper person. When displayed, it can carry labels or articles of clothing, or show parts of the body. It can then provide a talking point, a reading aid or part of a project on 'The body'.

Each outline could be developed into a character from a favourite story or play, or more lavishly detailed for a special historical display of dress or weapons – a Roman noblewoman, a Norman soldier, for example.

Paper figures can be particularly effective for a foyer display, to advertise special events or to display work about a visit.

Paper people

Age range
Three to thirteen.

Group size
Whole class,
small groups
or individuals.

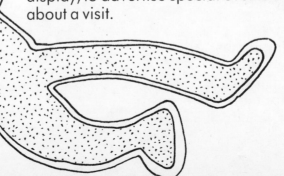

Mistakes

Age range
Seven to thirteen.

Group size
Whole class, pairs, individuals.

What you need
Chalk or marker, paper and pencils.

What to do
Write a sentence containing some errors on the board. The content can be related to topics you are working on, current stories or simple fun. It is helpful to state how many mistakes there are. The errors can be of grammar, punctuation, spelling, or a mixture, depending on the abilities of your class. Work through one or two sentences before the pupils try some on their own.

You can write sentences to highlight particular errors or to suit a particular child. The activity can also be turned into a game when needed.

The pupils write their corrected versions, either underlining the changes or using another colour.

It is useful to keep a collection of 'wrong' sentences in the back of your mark book. Write one on the board if some pupils finish ahead of the others, or you have a few minutes to fill. Children will enjoy this activity.
Sample sentences might be:

i am 6 mi nam is . . . (7)
Their are too egg in this Boxes. (5)
I sed i wood get im sum (6)
this is butiful speling. I lick it (5)
(*See copy page 117 for more sentences.*)

Comb painting

Age range
Three to eight.

Group size
Individuals, small groups.

cardboard
comb
brush

What you need
Poster paint and wallpaper paste mixed to a spreading consistency; large brushes; a collection of old plastic combs, or a variety of cardboard combs; aprons and covering for work surface; cartridge paper; scissors; pencils; rulers if children are to draw and cut their own combs.

What to do
Spread the paint and paste mixture all over the paper fairly thickly and evenly. Use a large brush. Lightly comb the paper, making patterns by varying the angle and direction of the comb. Do not let it degenerate into heavy scrubbing or card combs will bend too much, or possibly even disintegrate. One needs a light touch for artistic effects.

If older children make their own combs, you will need to show them how to mark and cut them out with pencil, ruler and scissors. It is a good skill practice activity. Alternatively, the day before, you could stick copies of the comb (*see copy page 118*) on to cardboard. Allow to dry.

Printing 1

Age range
Three to thirteen.

Group size
Whole class.

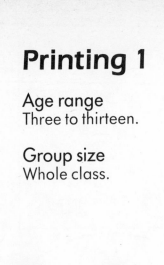

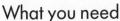

What you need
An assortment of corks, small blocks of wood, small jars, erasers, empty cotton reels, pencils, corrugated paper strips, potatoes, carrots, sprouts, scrap-paper for practice; plenty of paint made up in trays or saucers; covering-newspaper for surfaces; paper on which the patterns are to be printed. Do not make this too large. Cut A3 sheets into A4 or A5 sizes, as printing very small patterns can become tedious. Young children lose the notion of pattern and just dot the stamp about at random.

What to do
Ask the children to select one item to act as a stamp to print with. Demonstrate how to use it. Give out small sized sheets of paper – A5 for small stamps, A4 for larger ones. Encourage them to stamp their paper in neat, close lines.

Give out a sheet of A5 or A4 and show the pupils how to print in blocks of, say, fives. You can choose any number to act as useful reinforcement for number work.

The prints can also be used as borders, headings or bookmarks. Older pupils can cut their own stamps from potatoes or other vegetables with a knife. They may like to cut their own initials. Printing with fabric dyes on cloth can be an extension of this activity.

Printing 2

Age range
Three to thirteen.

Group size
Whole class or
small groups.

What you need
Leaves, paint, brushes (soft for painting,
stiff for stencilling), paper,
spray bottle, covering for work surface.

What to do
Leaf printing can follow on from topic work on trees or
seasons, and from relevant stories or poems.

You could take the pupils out for a walk to collect their
own leaves. Bark and leaf-rubbings can be one method
of recording their finds as part of a study of trees and
classification work in science. Children either select
leaves from your collection or sort out a set from their
own gathered on the walk.

There are two methods. For the first, carefully cover the
top surface of the leaf with paint. Press it face-down on
the paper, and use it as a printing stamp. Make one print
and leave space for writing. Alternatively, make many
prints and work up a pattern. For the second, place the
leaf on paper and hold it firmly. Dab a little paint all
round the leaf edge. This stencilling method is also
effective if paint is sprayed or flicked over the edges. Lift
the leaf off carefully to leave a clear white shape.

Both methods can be used with fabric dye on stretched
cotton material, or with coloured inks.

1 transfer print

2 stencil print

Masks 1

Age range
Five to seven.

Group size
Small groups.

What you need
Paper plates,
wool for hair,
paper,
adhesive tape,
ruler,
paint,
crayons,
pieces of material,
sponge,
glue.

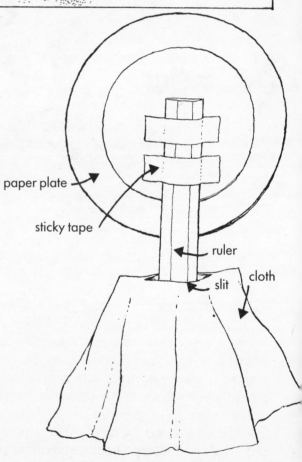

paper plate

sticky tape

ruler

slit

cloth

What to do

Prepare one mask to show the children. You might tell a story using the mask as a character. The children are then given a paper plate and colour in a face. Stick on wool for hair, or a piece of plastic sponge for a nose. Then tape a ruler on to the back of the plate. Features and curls cut out of paper can also be used. When the head is finished, take a piece of cloth and make a slit in the centre just wide enough to push the ruler through. Push the cloth up to the edge of the plate.

The finished masks can be used for storytelling and acting. Often, shy children will be helped to join in by using their mask as a front, and talking behind it.

Masks 2

Age range
Seven to nine.

Group size
Small groups.

What you need
Sugar paper, glue, string, scissors, scraps of wool, foil, sequins, feathers, paint, cereal packets.

basic template

What to do

Ask children to bring in large-sized cereal packets. Take a piece of sugar paper or the side of a cereal packet, and place it over a child's face. Carefully mark where the eye and mouth openings should be, and the height and width of the mask. Leave a little extra at the side for fastening. Draw a rough oval by joining up the outside marks, and make the eye and mouth openings. Cut round the oval. You should now have a basic template which the children can use to create their own masks. Show them, if necessary, how to cut out the eye and mouth openings. Each child can then paint and decorate his or her own mask, depending on what you are working on: witches, American Indians, clowns and space creatures, or characters in a story you are dramatising.

Fasten the masks on by making a small hole on either side and knotting a piece of string through, or by stapling on the ties. Groups of children can work together to produce masks for their own plays, and the masks can be displayed with any written work.

Filmstrips

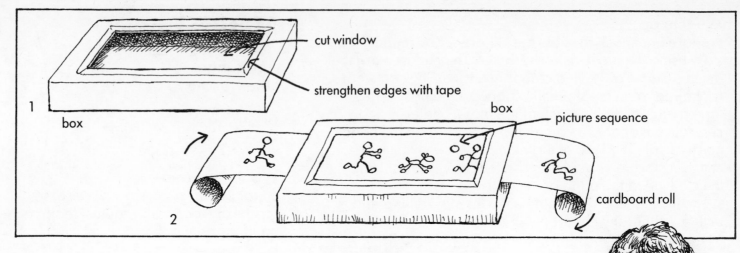

Age range
Eight to thirteen.

Group size
Small groups.

What you need
Box (the kind with fold-in ends that books are packed in is best), pencils, paints, felt tips, sticky tape, cardboard rolls, scissors.

What to do
Explain that the group is going to make a 'film-strip' – that is, a series of scenes or facts written and illustrated by them, and viewed one at a time. They could present a group topic in this way for the others in the class. Spend time deciding on the number of frames and the sequence. A director could be appointed. The box has a window cut out and the edges strengthened with tape. The size of the window will determine the size of the pictures or frames of the film-strip. This can be a continuous strip of paper cut to fit, or several sheets joined later into a roll. The children then write and draw their story or topic in frames which will fit the window in the box.

  When it is complete, fit the 'film' through the box. The ends can be attached to cardboard rolls to facilitate easy moving. Older children can produce a complete film-strip each.

Feely collage

'feely bag'

Age range
Three to eight.

Group size
Small groups or individuals.

What you need
Paper ready-cut and mounted, small pots of strong adhesive and applicators, cover for working surfaces, bag of assorted pasta shapes, small opaque containers each holding one kind of dried pulse or coloured pasta shapes. Try to obtain a good variety of textures and colours.

What to do

Ask children to come to you one at a time, and put their fingers in the 'feely' bag. They must then describe to the others what they can feel. When a number have had a try at describing and guessing the contents, reveal what is inside and explain that they are going to make designs using them. Show them one or two examples to illustrate what you mean.

Demonstrate ways of attaching pulses to paper. Small seeds are best sprinkled on to a glued area, and the surplus poured back into the container. Larger pasta pieces are best glued individually and pressed on.

Allow children to experiment, producing their own patterns or pictures. You could also suggest using this medium to illustrate a current topic. Some may find they like to draw their pattern first. Simple ideas such as fishes in tanks can be shapes from which less-skilled children can gain satisfaction and success.

This activity can be developed by the children into ideas for containers as presents – such as pencil holders or decorated boxes. You need clean tins or firm boxes, and ideally the finished object should be varnished.

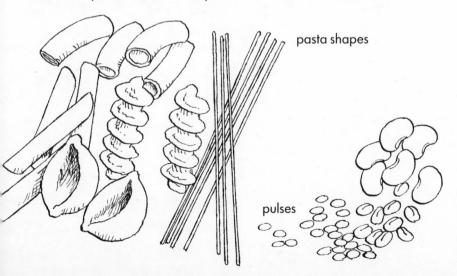

pasta shapes

pulses

Write a book

Age range
Nine to thirteen.

Group size
Small groups.

What you need
Paper,
pencils,
card,
nursery story-books,
scrap paper,
paints,
felt-tips.

What to do

Explain that the class are going to produce story-books for the infant classes. Look at those you have selected and elicit what the groups feel these stories have in common – clear print, simple stories, repetition, bright colours etc. Having established the criteria, the groups can then work to produce their own story, roughly planned on scrap paper first. Then the group has to decide what goes on each page, how much writing, what size drawing, what colours.etc. When the whole book, including cover design and title has been planned, the group produces the book on good paper with card covers. These can then be covered in clear plastic film. After being displayed, these books can be used in the infant classes – if the class will part with them!

Paper and pencil activities

Questionnaires and reports

Age range
Seven to thirteen.

Group size
Pairs.

What you need
Copy page 119.

What to do
Discuss previous listening activities which you may have done with the class, and explain that they are going to fill in some answers to questions about their listening habits. This is a self-evaluation exercise. The point is that if they listen carefully in lessons, they will learn more. A lot of people are not good listeners. How good are *they* at listening?

Give out copies of the questionnaire (*see* copy page 119) and help them fill in the boxes. All they have to do is tick the appropriate one.

When each pupil has completed their paper, ask the pupil next to them to read it and think about the answers. They should then write a report on what they read. This could be a simple matter of converting each question into a statement in its simplest form, or, more cleverly, summing up two or three answers in one sentence.

Show them the summary report below:

Stephen sits near the teacher in science lessons. He daydreams very little and often asks questions. He is easily put off by other pupils and prefers to talk in class than work. He is good at science but is always getting into trouble.

After the other pupil has completed the report on their partner, they should read it to him or her and check that it is accurate. It should only contain details from the questionnaire and not gratuitous information. The final version should be approved by both participants and signed by both as a true record.

At the end of the term or year, the questionnaire can be worked through again, and the pupils' study habits discussed with the teacher.

Friendly words

Age range
Seven to thirteen.

Group size
Individuals
or whole class.

What you need
Paper,
pencil,
copy page 120
(one for each pupil).

What to do
Discuss with the pupils words which they would use to refer to their friends or to describe friendly actions. For younger pupils make a list of some of these words on the board. Give out the copies of page 120. Ask them to discover how many friendly words they can find by moving across, down, diagonally, forwards or backwards.

Once the pupils know what to do, and have had several short practice sessions, record the best scores on a wall chart. Keep a note of each pupil's score in the teacher's record book.

Word search

Age range
Six to thirteen.

Group size
Whole class,
pairs or
individuals.

What you need
Paper,
pencils,
copy page 121.

What to do
Give the pupils a word search exercise such as the previous activity. Explain that they are now going to make up their own word searches for each other to do. If you select the topic of the word search, you can use it as an exercise to find out how much vocabulary they have retained. Encourage further study of it, and reinforce what they have learned in curriculum subject or topic areas.

First, each pupil has to make a list of words which relate to the topic they have studied. For example:

Topic: 'People who help us'

fireman/woman	ladder
nurse	plaster
doctor	operation
police officer	lost dog

They should then write these words across and down (or diagonally if they are able) in a matrix. Use copy page 121 or let them draw out their own. They should then fill in the rest of the matrix with other letters, to conceal them. They should count the number of words put into their matrix and write this at the side. When it is completed it can be swapped with someone else. Each then tries to unravel the other's word search. It can be a useful homework activity, once the pupils know what to do. It makes a more interesting method than rote learning. Finding words for their puzzles causes pupils to give more detailed and thoughtful attention to the texts they read.

matrix

A	Z	N	Q	P	W	N	Y	O	O	O	N	P	G	L
Z	C	D	F	E	J	U	L	K	O	R	S	S	N	O
M	M	G	V	F	I	R	E	M	A	N	W	V	P	S
G	H	I	L	L	H	S	M	O	Q	S	U	U	X	T
T	T	V	O	Q	P	E	P	S	S	T	Z	Y	R	D
P	O	L	I	C	E	O	F	F	I	C	E	R	S	O
T	B	E	B	E	W	Y	Z	M	P	D	Q	F	H	G
L	N	R	Z	U	F	M	P	Z	Z	O	A	C	B	E
O	Y	Z	T	V	I	J	K	Q	W	C	Y	W	A	O
O	P	E	R	A	T	I	O	N	T	T	N	B	B	D
D	R	A	M	N	T	I	O	X	P	O	N	Q	R	T
B	B	A	L	L	A	D	D	E	R	R	M	P	Q	S
Y	Z	T	T	V	F	G	D	O	N	G	L	O	P	S
P	L	A	S	T	E	R	U	T	Z	S	F	E	E	R

Scatter words and spiders

Age range
Seven to thirteen.

Group size
Individuals
or small group.

What you need
Paper,
pencils,
crayons,
felt-tip pens,
blackboard,
chalk.

What to do
Introduce a topic word, 'pets', for example. Ask for words related to that topic. These 'scatter words' can be written down all around the topic word.

Now ask the children for other words suitable for this treatment, and write a list on the blackboard. The children can then choose to develop a topic, singly or in groups. Examples might include: season, holidays, Christmas, school, my street, my hobby, my family.

Some children prefer to make word 'spiders' to help them remember important points. These have eight 'legs' extending from the central word.

When the children have produced their 'word scatters' in rough, they can space the words neatly on a new piece of paper, or make a word spider or spiders. These can be decorated round the border with a suitable design, or have the backgrounds tinted in and displayed. They can use these when they come to write about their topics.

Alphabet poems

Age range
Eight to thirteen.

Group size
Individuals,
pairs or
whole class.

What you need
Paper,
pencils,
copy page 122
(one for each pair).

What to do
Give out copies of page 122, one to each pair.
Alternatively, have the poem written on the board before
the lesson, or give it as a handwriting exercise at some
point. Explain the construction of the poem, with
reference to the alphabet, the fact that each first phrase
refers to a person, and that after each comma there is a
description of what that person did or was like. Note also
that the lines are rhymed in pairs. Explain that the poem
was written nearly 300 years ago by an anonymous man
or woman, and was probably chanted by children in
lessons to learn their alphabet, just as today some people
sing the alphabet to help remember its order.

The task the pupils are going to be set is to update this
poem to suit a modern learner.

Work on the first few lines together to show them what
to do, eg first list the alphabet down the paper

A
B
C
Next read out the first line, substituting someone modern
for Archer. Ask for the pupils' suggestions and write them
on the board, for example:

    A was an Android and lived in a shed.
    A was an 'Archer' and lived on a farm.
    A was an Android with wires in his head.

The first line is not very appropriate. The second comes
from a radio listener! The third line is probably the best.
Select the line preferred by most and move on to the next
one, rubbing out the others . . .
B was a Baker who sold all his bread,
C was a Chef, and cooked lovely meals,
D was a Driver who loved four wheels,
E was an Engineer . . .
F was a Farmer . . .
G was a . . .
The children should work on pairs of lines, trying first to
think of a person and then filling in one line after the
other. Some pairs of lines will suddenly fit. More often,
there are awkward spaces, and a lot of mental work to
do. Ideas can be better generated when pairs work
together. After the first session, the poem can be worked
on at intervals over several days. It can serve as a useful
five-minute filler.

It will probably be possible to make only one complete
poem, taking the best ideas from all the groups. When
the easy lines have been completed, dictionaries will help
with unusual words. In the end, the children may have to
use some of the original lines to complete their poems.
Do not let the task go uncompleted. Finish off after about
a week, with each pupil filling in their gaps from the
original poem.

Secret sentences

Age range
Seven to thirteen.

Group size
Pairs.

What you need
Pencils,
paper,
copy page 123 (optional).

What to do
Explain to the class that when we listen we often fail to remember all the details of what someone says. The more they say, the more difficult it is for us to remember it all. In lessons, children more often remember jokes and practical examples or personal details, and forget the main ideas or the really important facts.

To check this out, each pupil should invent and write down a six-word sentence. They should then read it to their partner. The partner then has to repeat the sentence back to the reader, with all words correct and in the right order. The reader should record any changes noted.

Next, each of the pair invents and writes down an 11-word sentence, and reads this to their partner for immediate recall. Each takes a turn at reading and listening, and records the results.

The teacher should compile a list of omissions and errors collected from the class, to discover their nature. There should not be too many errors at this stage.

The teacher should then give out a copy of, for example, the following 21-word sentence to one of each of the pairs in the class:

The teacher placed the 35 little green marbles on the side table, turned round to the class and began the talk.

If you have any poor readers, make sure they are paired with good readers who can read out the long sentence. Poor writers and spellers can whisper their sentence to the teacher, and gain help in writing them down.

Each pupil should draw a table or be given a copy of page 123 to record errors of the class.

It is possible to make histograms of the most frequent errors. The most important thing is for the pupils to be able to see which words are changed, and to try to puzzle out why. The middle words are less well remembered on the whole than beginnings and ends. Sometimes a person may lose the sense of the passage altogether. Others will give a much shortened version, which preserves the main sense. This latter shows a good grasp, a brain which is working well and efficiently. Sometimes, however, abbreviation can distort the meaning of the sentence. Warn the children of this.

Excuses

Age range
Seven to thirteen.

Group size
Whole class
or groups.

What you need
Chalk,
paper,
pencil.

What to do
Discuss occasions when excuses are required – lost
articles or money; forgotten books, trainers or gym kit;
being late; talking at wrong time; work not completed
etc. Suggest really good excuses that could be invented –
excuses which are long-winded or funny, involving a
series of accidents or coincidences.

Ask the class to make up excuses individually or in
groups. When they are elaborate or funny enough they
are to be told as convincingly as possible. Good excuses
can be written down, illustrated and displayed.

Words to avoid

Age range
Eight to thirteen.

Group size
Whole class
or group.

What you need
Blackboard,
large sheet of paper,
paper,
pencil,
copy page 124.

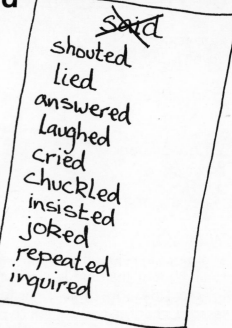

What to do
When talking about how to write stories, draw attention
to the over-use of 'said'. Give a simple example of how
changing 'said' to 'shouted' or 'pleaded' etc can make
stories more interesting.

Ask what words could be used instead of always using
'said'? Write some on the board, and collect as many
more as possible. Check that the children understand
them by asking them to give you examples of how they
would use them. These words can be written out on a
large sheet of paper by a group of children, and added
to as they find more. Either individually or in groups, the
children can now write a story using dialogue but
avoiding the word 'said'.

See copy page 124 for some sample practice
sentences. This activity can also apply to other words
such as 'went' as well.

Word squares

Age range
Eight to thirteen.

Group size
Whole class.

What you need
Scrap paper,
chalk,
paper,
pencils,
blank grids
(copy page 125).

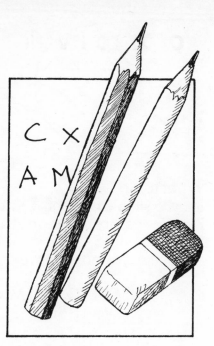

What to do
Draw out a grid on the blackboard (a). Fill in three letters and ask the pupils to fill in the rest of the squares, so that the lines read the same across and down. When they have successfully completed (a), try them with (b).

(a)

C		
	L	
		D

C	A	T
A	L	E
T	E	D

(b)

B			
	V		
		A	
			S

B	O	R	E
O	V	E	N
R	E	A	D
E	N	D	S

They can then try on their own, and build up a class collection.

Some pupils will need more guidance. Work through an example with them to show what is meant, or give them the first line across and down.

S	L	A	M
L	A	C	E
A	C	H	E
M	E	E	T

M	O	S	S
O	V	A	L
S	A	G	A
S	L	A	M

C	A	R	E
A	R	E	A
R	E	A	R
E	A	R	L

G	R	A	B
R	O	V	E
A	V	E	R
B	E	R	T

Codes

Age range
Seven to thirteen.

Group size
Individuals
or groups.

What you need
Codes,
prepared messages,
alphabet (copy page 126),
paper,
pencils,
lemon juice
and iron
(optional).

Psst! UOYH TIWSK OOBSA
EDITH GIRBYN ATHGU
OBU OYEV AH ?

What to do
Show a simple code on board: A = 1, B = 2, C = 3 . . .
Z = 26. Then try a few words: 3,1,18; 5,1,18,19;
23,5,12,12; 4,15,14,5.

If that seems easy, move on to code number 2:

ABCDEFGHIJKLMNOPQRSTUVWXYZ
ZYXWVUTSRQPONMLKJIHGFEDCBA

● or code number three:

ABCDEFGHIJKLMNOPQRSTUVWXYZ
CDEFGHIJKLMNOPQRSTUVWXYZAB

● or code number four:

TIW ONK UO YECNOY SAESI TI

(messages written backwards and letter groupings
rearranged).

When those codes that you have decided are suitable
for your class have been mastered, they can make up
their own messages and codes. If they write them in
lemon juice, they'll be invisible until ironed!

When deciphering codes, it is useful to know the
frequency with which letters appear. This is the order off
frequency: E T A INSO H R D L U CM F WY PG B V K Q
JX Z.

Word wheel

Age range
Six to ten.

Group size
Individuals
or small groups.

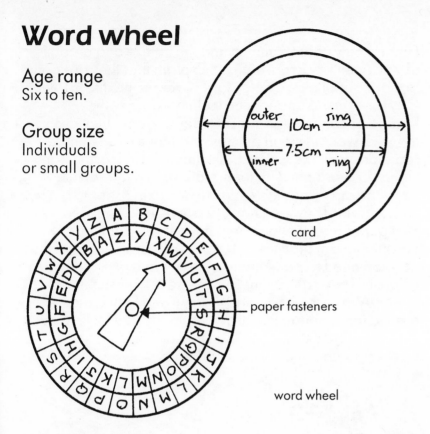

card

paper fasteners

word wheel

What you need
Pieces of circular card about 10 cm in diameter and a
paper fastener 7.5 cm in diameter; pen.

What to do
Draw a circle 10 cm across on a piece of card. Draw
another circle 7.5 cm across on the same piece of card.
Write the letters of the alphabet, in order, around the
outer circle, spaced out regularly. Letter the inner circle,
using the alphabet in reverse. Make a red arrow, and
fasten it in the centre with a paper fastener. The children
can then make up some messages to send to each other
which have to be decoded.

How many squares?

Age range
Seven to twelve.

Group size
Individuals.

What you need
Copy page 127 ,
pencils.

What to do
Hand out the copies of page 127.

There are 16 single squares, one large square, nine
containing four squares each, and four containing nine
squares each, a total of 31.

Ask the children to find as many squares as they can.

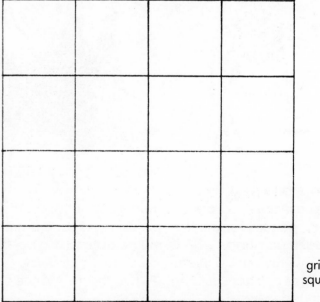

grid of
squares

School news

Age range
Seven to thirteen.

Group size
Groups of two or three.

What you need
One cassette recorder and microphone (optional); paper, pencils for the first few sessions; one blank tape for each pair (most pupils will be able to provide their own, but they are a useful investment); even tapes and cassettes are not essential. A 'live' performance could be arranged instead.

What to do
Discuss news programmes and the nature and purposes of documentary programmes. Explain that they are going to learn about a particular topic over the next few weeks (any topic in the normal curriculum would suffice). Instead of compiling a topic folder or book, they are going to work in small groups and make a ten minute radio programme instead. Ask them to look in the Radio Times, or work out with them from such a magazine, which programmes they might listen to in order to get the feel of them. They then have to convert the knowledge they gain about the topic into interviews, running commentaries, playlets and sound effects. The ideas they develop need to be written down as each group decides on them. They can use these notes to rehearse their scenes. When they are ready, they need to find a quiet area to tape their next extract. Many children will take their tapes home and continue to work on them there, where they can control the conditions.

Follow-up
As the tapes are completed, set aside ten minutes after morning break and lunchtime to settle down and listen to them.

Picture stories

Age range
Four to twelve.

Group size
Individuals
or groups.

What you need
Paper,
colouring pens
or crayons.

What to do
The children can tell some stories without using any words, just a sequence of pictures. They could also show *how to do* something in pictures only, for example: 'How to make a cup of tea', 'How to get ready for a game of football/netball'. Lead on to a discussion about visual codes and symbols: flags, computer symbols, smoke signals etc.

Outdoor Activities

Traffic lights

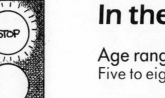

Age range
Eight to eleven.

Group size
Whole class.

What you need
An equal number of red, yellow and green cards (coloured on one side only) for each team; boxes to put used cards in; a starting and finishing line.

What to do
Put the class into teams of equal number, behind a starting line. Place the cards at a distance, face down with the box next to them. Provide one set for each team.

The first runner from each team runs to the cards and picks up the top one, looks at it and puts it in the box.

Stop
If it is red, she or he runs back to team. When she or he has crossed the starting line, the next one goes.

Wait
If it is yellow, she or he puts it in the box, shouts 'Next!' and waits there. She or he can run to the end line when a team-mate chooses green.

Go
If it is green, she or he runs to the end line. When he or she has crossed it, the next one in the team tries. The first team home wins.

The purpose of this game is to encourage speed of response and alertness to the signals. Similar games using the three colour cards are easily invented.

In the sea

Age range
Five to eight.

Group size
Whole class or groups.

What you need
Large circle or line on floor.

What to do
The children all stand on one side of the line, or outside the circle. The purpose is for them to listen carefully and then respond by moving or not moving to the call. When you call 'In the sea!' they all jump over the line. When you call 'on the shore!' they all jump back over the line. When this pattern is established, you then call 'On the sea!' or 'In the shore' and try to catch them out. After a few trials you then play the game properly. Those who jump at the wrong time are 'out'.

Compass game

Age range
Eight to eleven.

Group size
Small groups (five or nine).

What you need
Chalk.

What to do
Draw a compass: four points for younger children, eight points for older ones.

A child stands on each point and one in the centre. You call out two points, and the children standing on them try to change places before the one in the middle can get there. The one who doesn't make it to the new place goes into the middle. The children should count the number of times each one is made to stay in the middle. The game encourages listening and responding together with the rapid movements suitable for practising ball skills.

Statues

Age range
Five to eight.

Group size
Whole class, divided into two or three groups.

What you need
Large space (outdoors or indoors).

What to do
Draw a starting line, or point, about one metre from the person who is 'it', who stands facing a wall or fence. This person turns at intervals to look at the approaching line of figures. As 'it' turns, the others must 'freeze' and become 'statues'. When 'it' turns back to the wall, they must try to creep forward again. When 'it' looks at them, if they move or quiver they are 'out'. They then stand and watch and help 'it' judge the others.

This will help improve concentration, responsiveness, and balance and control skills in young children. Children less successful in reading and writing tasks have a chance to shine here. Make them feel skills such as being able to predict the actions of other people from slight movements are also valued and important.

Snow detectives

Age range
Three to seven;
seven to thirteen.

Group size
For younger children: divide the class into groups of three; one group goes out, and comes back to report to another group of three.
For older children: divide the class into pairs. Work with no more than half the class at one time in both cases.

What you need
Snow, five waterproof objects of different shapes and sizes for younger children; ten objects for older children, as well as pencils and squared paper. Make a list of the objects on the blackboard or on a piece of paper. You will need parent or helper to keep an eye on the group outside, if you cannot be with them or observe them through the window.

What to do
As soon as snow starts to fall, go out and 'plant' the objects in a suitable area of the playground or grassed space. Allow the snow to cover the objects. The idea is that when the snow stops, the children have to go out to discover and identify the objects.
   They must follow the rules:
1 The objects must not be uncovered or touched in any way.
2 Each of the five (or ten) objects has to be correctly identified whilst still under the snow.
3 The object and its position must be plotted, and reported back to a group inside. They must listen carefully or read the instructions, and then go out to find the objects.
4 'Plotters' and 'finders' should take turns with each task.

The **younger children** should, on finding an object, discuss how they will explain it to the group inside. They then go inside to find their group and give their explanations. They can follow their group out and watch, but must not give any more clues or help. After this practice they should try the other four objects, with the same two teams switching places and given two turns each. Young children need such opportunities to practise explaining and giving instructions for others to follow.

If squared paper is given out to **older children**, each square can represent steps. Co-ordinates can be plotted for each object, so that treasure or detective maps can be made for each object.
   After one or two have been plotted, the other group can be given the maps to follow. Their task will be to check the reliability of the instructions. They can collect up the objects when all the maps have been verified.

Nature map

Age range
Seven to ten.

Group size
Small groups.

What you need
Pencils,
paper,
clipboards,
several sheets of white cloth
or cartridge paper,
several rulers
or short sticks.

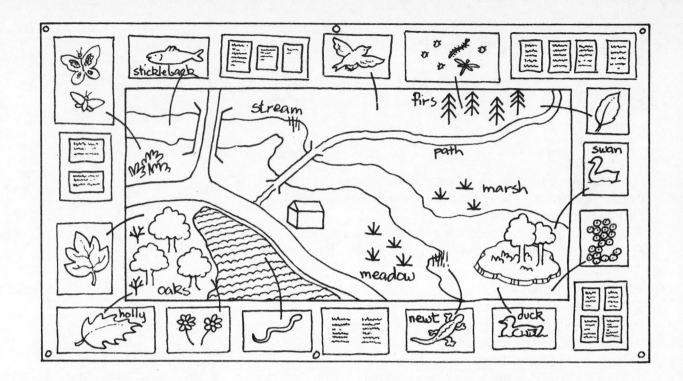

What to do
Choose an area, perhaps a park or a nearby open space that offers a choice of habitats. It is a good idea to investigate the area beforehand so you can direct the groups' observations.

Explain to your groups that you are going out to observe animals and insects and where they live, but *not* to collect them. Discuss what they think they might do and see, and what signs to look for, such as things on the ground; bark on trees; watching the sky, bushes and trees; larger animal tracks; trails etc.

White cloth can be used to make a 'minibeast' survey. Four children hold the cloth under a bush, whilst a fifth one shakes and taps the branches – ten taps should do. They should then identify and count the minibeasts which fall out, before they scuttle away. The rest should be put

back around or on the bush.

The groups can write down their findings on paper, taking care to specify exactly what they saw, and where. You can, if you wish, provide a simple plan of the area and/or a questionnaire to direct their observations.

The information can be shared by each group telling the others what they observed, or writing a report for a 'nature news sheet' or display.

Follow-up
Make a larger map of the area. Label or number on the map the habitats and plant or animal life observed. Underneath or around the map, attach the related drawings and written work. The activity can be part of a project on conservation or map-making.

Litter studies

Age range
Ten to thirteen.

Group size
Small groups.

What you need
Plastic bags or bin liners,
rubber gloves or
disposable plastic gloves,
paper,
pencils,
newspaper.

plastic gloves

bin liner

What to do
Decide on an area suitable for this experiment, such as the playground or a street. Explain to the groups that they are conducting an experiment into the kinds and amount of litter to be found in one area. They are to pick up the litter, wearing protective gloves, and put it in the plastic bags.

When the litter has been collected, place newspaper over a large table or some desks, and sort the litter into piles – paper, cans, plastic etc.

You can then discuss the sources of the litter. Which shops did it come from? What were the reasons for the litter? Were there enough litter bins? or was it due to carelessness? What kinds of litter were there – biodegradable/dangerous/unpleasant? Discuss the problems of litter; costs of removal, where it occurs most, how unsightly or unhealthy it is. What possible solutions are there – penalties/education/campaigns?

poster

items	corners	under trees	beside bin	playground
10				
9				
8				
7				
6				
5				
4				
3				
2				
1				

graph

Follow-up
Make a display, using posters and graphs of the amount of litter found, and the children's written work. The activity can be developed into a project on pollution and conservation.

Tag games

Age range
Six to eleven.

Group size
Whole class.

What you need
Bands.

What to do
Have one 'catcher' for every ten children. The catcher should be distinguished by a coloured band, or a handkerchief tied round their arm. Everyone runs around, without bumping into each other. The catchers have to 'tag' as many as possible within a set time, say while you count slowly to ten. You can ask how many were 'tagged'. If some were not, then choose your new catcher from those.

The catcher must learn to 'tag' lightly, and how to change direction often so that they can catch children unexpectedly. They must also learn to be aware of the other catcher/s so that they maximise their efforts. The other children must learn to dodge, keep moving, and keep a look-out for all the catchers.

There are numerous variations of tag games and children often know versions that you may not be aware of.

When you stop the game the catcher hands his or her band to the nearest person, who then becomes the catcher. The catcher tries to pass the band on while the other children dodge to avoid it. When caught, that child takes the band.

- **Pairs:** catchers work in twos, holding inside hands. When either catches a player, that catcher changes places.
- **Freeze tag:** when caught, the player must freeze until everyone is caught – or you stop the game.
- **Sun and frost:** the catchers wear yellow or blue bands (yellow = Sun; blue = Frost). 'Frost' freezes the players, who must remain immobile unless touched by the 'Sun', who releases them.
- **Tunnel tag:** when caught, the player stands with feet wide apart. They are only released when a free player crawls under their legs.
- **Tree tag:** the caught players stretch their arms out like a tree. They can only be released if another player runs all round them, under their 'branches'.
- **Leapfrog tag:** the caught players crouch down. They are only released when a free player puts his or her hands on their backs and leaps over them.
- **Tail tags:** everyone has a band to tuck into the back of their shorts, like a tail. When you give the signal, the players try to gather the tails of the others while trying to prevent their own being collected (they are not allowed to hold their tails in place). You can find who has collected the most tails, or has not lost his or hers, if you wish. This game can be played in groups. For example (1) Twos: one tries to take the tail while the other dodges sideways – not backwards – to prevent him or her. (2) Threes, fours: One child has the tail and is joined either in a ring or a snake to the others. One catcher tries to get the tail but the group work together to dodge the 'tail' away.

Chalk a shape

Age range
Five to nine.

Group size
Small groups.

What you need
Playground,
chalk,
measuring tapes,
wooden measures,
trundle wheel.

What to do
Discuss with the children the relative sizes of dinosaurs and other animals, or sizes of giants in various stories. In order to increase their awareness of size, go into the playground and let the children chalk out (using the measures) the various shapes of 'giants' or 'dinosaurs'.

Shadow images

Age range
Five to seven.

Group size
Individuals
or small groups.

What you need
Sunshine,
camera,
objects of various shapes.

What to do
Photograph the shadow of various objects which are familiar to the children, outside their usual setting. Examples might include a chair, a desk, a bike, a climbing frame. The children have to guess from the photographed shadow what the object is and which way it is facing.

Follow-up
Photograph children who have a distinctive shadow, for example a child with a pony-tail hairstyle. See if the other children can guess which child's shadow is on the picture. These activities can lead on to making shadow puppets, or discussion about light and dark, etc.

Shine a light

Age range
Three to nine.

Group size
Individuals.

What you need
Sunshine,
mirrors*,
a wall,
chalk.

What to do
Ask the children to hold a mirror in different positions, in order to find out what they can see. Can they see around corners, over fences, under bushes? Encourage the children to talk about their findings.

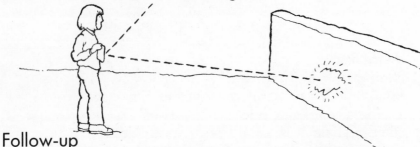

Follow-up
Draw a line on a wall. Encourage the children to reflect a spot of sunlight with a mirror. Can the children follow the line with the 'spot'? The children could play a game of 'tag' with each other. One child tries to 'catch' another child's 'spot', by using their mirrors.

* Galt sell plastic mirrors which can be cut into different shapes.

Stars boxes

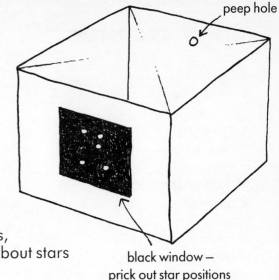

peep hole

black window —
prick out star positions

Age range
Seven to thirteen.

Group size
Individuals.

What you need
Empty boxes
(preferably cuboid),
paper, chalk or pencils,
scissors, glue, books about stars
(in a sturdy box).

What to do
Cut a square about 15 cm square from one end of a box, and paste a patch of black paper over it. Ask the children to keep a look-out from their bedroom windows each night. When it gets dark they should copy down a group or constellation of stars.

Do not tell the children about what sort of structure to look for, but talk about shapes or patterns which seem to belong together. Ask the children to record the patterns in chalk on their box, and check it over several evenings. They should then cut tiny holes where the chalk-marks are. A peephole about 3 mm across should be cut opposite the black back-screen to view the constellation.

When all the children have made a star box, books on the constellations should then be collected and brought in. A session can be spent poring over the books and charts to see if they can find their patterns. This enables them to work in the same kind of way as astronomers in ancient times. They can search for and retell stories which relate to their constellation.

Colourful kite

Age range
Five to eight.

Group size
Individuals.

What you need
Ceiling tiles,
scissors,
felt-tip pens,
rubber band,
coloured crêpe paper,
knitting needle,
string, two buttons,
ball of string.

What to do
Mark the centre of a ceiling tile with a dot. Make another dot 12 cm from the centre of the tile. Use a knitting needle to make holes in the dots you have marked. Make sure the holes are big enough for string to go through. Cut a piece of string approximately 40 cm long, and tie a knot at one end. This is the 'bridle'. Thread a button on to the string. Thread a second button on to the string and tie a knot in the end. Loop a rubber band on to the string, and pull the loop tight when the band is in the middle of the bridle. Tie the end of a ball of string to the rubber band.

Cut strips of crêpe paper 5 cm wide. Use sticky tape to stick the streamers to the kite. Now cut your tile into a shape and colour a face on it.

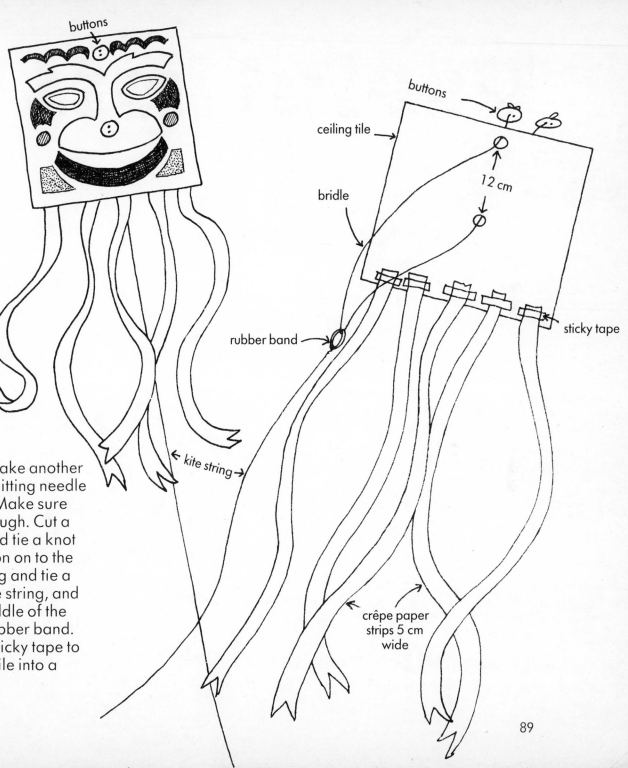

buttons

buttons

ceiling tile

12 cm

bridle

rubber band

sticky tape

kite string

crêpe paper strips 5 cm wide

Useful lists

Outing list

Sticky labels for names
Spare set of unisex clothes
Spare set of pants
Vomit bags
Tissues
Cotton wool
Bandage, gauze (elasticated)
Plastic sheeting to sit on
Plastic cups
Small container of fresh water
Safety pins
Plastic bags for rubbish and soiled clothing
A shopping trolley saves carrying a heavy bag!

Make sure all participants and helpers know where to assemble for lunch, where toilets are and where to meet for the homeward journey.

Always take the licence number of the coach and the telephone number of your school.

Remember that helpers will not be as familiar as you are with all the children's names. A list of the children in their care is important.

Do not put plasters on injuries: children may be allergic. Do not administer aspirin or other drugs. If in doubt, obtain advice at a local medical centre.

Make your own list of useful addresses

---

1 Local Teachers' Centre:

Name:
Address:

Telephone number:

---

2 Education Offices:

Special Needs Adviser:
Primary Adviser:
Advisory Teacher:
Peripatetic Teacher:
Address:

Telephone number:

---

3 Local Hospital:

Hospital Teacher(s):
Hospital:
Children's Ward:
Address:

Telephone number:

---

4 Drug Abuse Centre:
5 NSPCC Help Line:
6 Social Services Help Line:
7 Careers Advisory Service/Information:

---

8 Police Station number:
9 Community Police Officer:
10 Social Services Dept.:
Education Welfare Officer:

---

11 Other useful local contacts
Remedial Centre:
Museums:
Local farms which welcome visits:

---

12 Local University/Polytechnic/College of Higher Education for in-service help or information:

Contact names:

---

13 Library Services:

---

14 Saturday Clubs (eg NAGC 'Explorers' Clubs'):

New Information Centres:

This page may be photocopied for use in the classroom and should not be declared in any return in respect of any photocopying licence.

Useful addresses for information

Amateur Music
Association
Medlock School
Wadeson Road
MANCHESTER
M13 9UR
Gen. Sec. A Jurgis

Association for
Industrial
Archaeology
c/o Ironbridge Gorge
Museum
IRONBRIDGE
Telford
Shropshire
Sec. A P Stephens

Association for
Science Education
College Lane
HATFIELD
Hertfordshire
AL10 9AA
Sec. B G Atwood

Association for Study
of the Curriculum
Bishop Grosseteste
College
Newport
LINCOLN LN1 3DY
Hon. Sec. Jean
Whittaker

Association of School
Natural History
Societies
Lancing College
LANCING
West Sussex
BN15 0RW
Sec. G W Shaw

British Association for
the Advancement of
Science
Fortress House
23 Savile Row
LONDON W1X 1AB
Sec. Dr D W Morley

The British
Association for Early
Childhood Education
Studio 3/2
140 Tabernacle Street
LONDON EC2 4SD
Sec. Mrs B G Boon

The British
Astronomical
Association
Burlington House
Piccadilly
LONDON W1V 9AG
Sec. Mrs F A Moore

British Diabetic
Association
10 Queen Anne Street
LONDON W1M 0BD
Sec. D Armitage CBE

British Dyslexic
Association
98 London Road
READING
Berks RG1 5AU
Admin.: Mrs J Smith

British Epilepsy
Association
Anstey House
40 Hanover Square
LEEDS LS3 1BE

British Petroleum
Education Service
PO Box 5
WETHERBY
West Yorkshire
LS23 7EW

British Schools
Exploring Society
c/o Royal
Geographical Society
1 Kensington Gore
LONDON SW7 2AR
Sec. Miss P A Arden

British Waterways
Board
Melbury House
Melbury Terrace
LONDON NW1 6JX

Central Office of
Information
Hercules Road
Westminster Bridge
LONDON SE1 7DU

Commission for
Racial Equality
Elliot House
10–12 Allington Street
LONDON SW1E 5EH
Dir. Pete Newsom

Community Service
Volunteers' Advisory
Service
237 Pentonville Road
LONDON N1 9NJ
National
Co-ordinator: Ann
Griffith

Consumers'
Association
14 Buckingham Street
LONDON
WC2N 6DS
Senior Press Officer:
Val Bethell

Countryside
Commission
John Dower House
Crescent Place
CHELTENHAM
Glos. GL50 3RA
Publications
department

Department of Energy
Information Division
Thames House South
Millbank
LONDON SW1P 4QJ

Duke of Edinburgh
Award
5 Prince of Wales
Terrace
LONDON W8 5PG
Dir. Robert Heron

Equal Opportunities
Commission
Overseer's House
Quay Street
MANCHESTER
M3 3HN

English Schools'
Athletic Association
26 Coniscliffe Road
STANLEY
Co. Durham DH9 7RF
Hon. Sec. N Dickinson

The Folklore Society
c/o University College
London
Gower Street
LONDON WC1E 6BT
Hon. Sec. A R Vickery

Keep Britain Tidy
Group
Bostel House
37 West Street
BRIGHTON BN1 2RE
D J Lewis

Learning Difficulties
Research Project
Kingston Polytechnic
Gipsy Hill Centre
Kingston Hill
KINGSTON-UPON-
THAMES
Surrey KT2 7LB
Dir. Diane
Montgomery

Leverhulme Trust
15–19 New Fetter
Lane
LONDON EC4A 1NR
Dir. Sir Rex Richards
DSC FRS

Milk Marketing Board
of England and Wales
THAMES DITTON
Surrey KT7 0EL

MIND (National
Association for
Mental Health)
22 Harley Street
LONDON W1N 2ED
Dir. C Heginbotham

Microelectronics
Education Support
Unit
Advanced
Technology Building
Science Park
University of Warwick
COVENTRY
West Midlands
CV4 7EZ

National Association
for Gifted Children
1 South Audley Street
LONDON W1Y 5DQ
Dir. E J G Welch

National Association
for Remedial
Education
2 Litchfield Road
STAFFORD ST17 4JX
Gen. Sec. Roy Cooper

National Association
for the Welfare of
Children in
Hospital
Argyle House
29/31 Euston Road
LONDON NW1 2SD
Dir. Jean Lovell-Davis

National Association
of Youth Orchestras
Ainslie House
11 St Colme Street
EDINBURGH
EH3 6AG
Sec. Carol Main

National Autistic Society
276 Willesden Lane
LONDON NW2 5RB
Gen. Sec.
Mrs M White

National Children's Bureau
8 Wakeley Street
LONDON EC1V 7QE
Dir. R Davie
PhD FBPSS

National Council for Special Education
1 Wood Street
STRATFORD-UPON-AVON
Warwickshire
CV37 6JE

National Deaf Children's Society
45 Hereford Road
LONDON W2 5AH
Dir. Dr Carry Cayton
BA BPhil

National Federation for Educational Research
The Mere
Upton Park
SLOUGH SL1 2DQ
Dir. Dr Clare Burstall
BA FBPSS

National Trust
36 Queen Anne's Gate
LONDON SW1 9AS

Natural Energy Association
2 York Street
LONDON W1 1PA

Post Office Users' National Council
Waterloo Bridge House
Waterloo Road
LONDON SE1 8UA

Royal Society for the Prevention of Accidents (RoSPA)
Cannon House
The Priory
Queensway
BIRMINGHAM
B4 6BS
Sec. M M T Ward

Royal Society for the Prevention of Cruelty to Animals
Causeway
HORSHAM
West Sussex
RH12 1HG
HQ Ed. Office: Cindy Millburn BSc MI Biol

Royal Society for the Protection of Birds (RSPB)
The Lodge
SANDY
Bedfordshire
SG19 2DL
Head of Education:
David Elcome M Sc

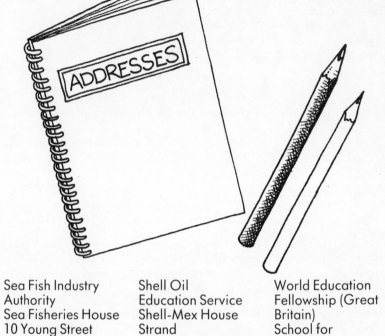

Sea Fish Industry Authority
Sea Fisheries House
10 Young Street
EDINBURGH
EH2 4JQ

SENSE (The National Deaf, Blind & Rubella Assoc.)
311 Gray's Inn Road
LONDON WC1X 8PT
Dir. Rodney Clark

Shell Oil Education Service
Shell-Mex House
Strand
LONDON WC2R 0DX

Wildflower Society
68 Outwoods Road
LOUGHBOROUGH
Leics LE11 3LY

World Education Fellowship (Great Britain)
School for Independent Studies
North East London Polytechnic
Holbrook Road
LONDON E15 3EA
Hon. Sec. Hazel Cross

Ten recommended books — older age range

Tom's Midnight Garden Philippa Pearce
Charlotte's Web E B White
Ghost of Thomas Kempe Penelope Lively
Terrible Term of Tyke Tyler Gene Kempe
Third Class Genie Robert Leeson
The Dragon in the Garden Reginald Maddock
Stig of the Dump Clive King
Carrie's War Nina Bawden
The Machine Gunners Robert Westall
Secret Garden Frances H Burnett

Ten recommended books for reading to 5–8 year olds

Gumdrop Stories Val Biro
Play School Stories (BBC/Knight)
Days with Frog and Toad Arnold Lobel
Little Old Mrs Pepperpot Alf Prøysen
The Owl Who Was Afraid of the Dark Jill Tomlinson
James and the Giant Peach Roald Dahl
The Fox Busters Dick King-Smith
Our Best Stories ed Anne Wood and Ann Pilling
My Naughty Little Sister Stories Dorothy Edwards
The Julian Stories Ann Cameron

Useful poetry anthologies

Fives, sixes and sevens Warne 1968
Gargling with Jelly Brian Patten, Puffin 1986
I Like this Poem ed Kaye Webb, Puffin 1979
Illustrated Treasury of Poetry for Children ed David Ross, Collins 1978
Junior Voices ed Geoffrey Summerfield, Penguin
Marbles in My Pocket ed Moira Andrew, Macmillan 1986
Mind Your Own Business Michael Rosen, Deutsch 1974
Over the Bridge ed John Loveday, Puffin 1981
Oxford Book of Children's Verse sel. Joan & Peter Opie, OUP 1973
Please Mrs Butler Allan Ahlberg, Kestrel 1983
Poems for 7 years and under ed Helen Nicoll Kestrel 1983
Poetry Workshop Michael & Peter Benton, EUP 1975
Quick, Let's Get Out of Here Michael Rosen & Quentin Blake, Puffin 1985
Round about Six sel. Margaret G Rawlins, Warne 1973
Round about Ten sel. Geoffrey Palmer, Noel Lloyd, Warne
Say it Again Granny John Agard, Bodley Head
Sky in the Pie Roger McGough, Kestrel 1984
The Children's Book of Comic Verse sel. Christopher Logue, Batsford 1979
The Faber Book of Nursery Songs sel. Donald Mitchel, Faber 1968
The Merry Go Round sel. James Reeves, Puffin 1969
The Rattle Bag Seamus Heaney and Ted Hughes, Faber 1982
Times Delight Raymond Wilson, Hamlyn 1977

Story poems

The Golden Vanity Anonymous
The Ballad of Sir Patrick Spens Anonymous
Widdecombe Fair Anonymous
The Wraggle-Taggle Gipsies Anonymous
The Jackdaw of Rheims R H Barham
Jim Hilaire Belloc
Mathilda Hilaire Belloc
Henry King Hilaire Belloc
The Pied Piper of Hamelin Robert Browning
John Gilpin William Cowper
The Yarn of 'Nancy Bell' W S Gilbert
Tom's Bomb David Hornsby
The Owl and the Pussycat Edward Lear
The Wreck of the Hesperus H W Longfellow
Bold Robin Thomas Love Peacock
A Legend of Lake Okeefinokee Laura E Richards
The Peacock and the Man from Mars Paul Roche
Lochinvar Sir Walter Scott
Mother Knows Best R C Scriven
Little Billee W M Thackeray
Dad and the Cat and the Tree Kit Wright
My Party Kit Wright

Spells and enchantments

The Puffin Book of Magic Verse chosen by Charles Causley, 1974
Hallowe'en Leonard Clark
Hallowe'en Eleanor Farjeon
Hallowe'en John Kitching
Hallowe'en Marie Lawson
Lazy Witch Myra Cohn Livingstone
Lollocks Robert Graves
The Witch Percy H Ilott
Wicked Witch's Kitchen X J Kennedy
The Witches Ride Karla Kuskin
The Blob Wes Magee
The Witch's Brew Wes Magee
The Listeners Walter de la Mare
Some One Walter de la Mare
Witch Goes Shopping Lilian Moore
Witch's Menu Sonia Nikolay
Space Travellers James Nimmo
The Magical House Kenneth Patchen
The Wee Woolly Witchie of Whistlewood Way Jack Prelutsky
Countdown Jack Prelutsky
Old Moll James Reeves
Two Witches Alexander Resnikoff
Midnight Wood Raymond Wilson

Animal poems

Penguin Book of Animal Verse ed George McBeth, 1965
The Yak Hilaire Belloc
Parrot Alan Brownjohn
Chameleon Alan Brownjohn
Rabbit and Dragon Tony Charles
The Mole Stanley Cook
Mr Jonas is Cool Jeni Couzyn
The Centipede's Song Roald Dahl
The Tigress Clifford Dyment
Fox Clifford Dyment
Cats Eleanor Farjeon
The Heron Gregory Harrison
Farm Cat Paul Hyland
Pigeons Richard Kell
The Zebra James Kirkup
My Gerbil John Kitching
Bat D H Lawrence
Tyrannosaurus Rex Wes Magee
Rhamphorynchus Wes Magee
The Fly Walter de la Mare
Frogs Norma McCaig
Puppy and I A A Milne
Milk for the Cat Harold Monroe
The Tale of Custard the Dragon Ogden Nash
The Hippopotamus Jack Prelutsky
Cows James Reeves
The Caterpillar Christina Rosetti
The Meadow Mouse Theodore Roethke
The Serpent Theodore Roethke
The Sloth Theodore Roethke
The Eagle Alfred Lord Tennyson
Amber Shirley Toulson
Hedgehog A Thwaite
The Swallows Andrew Young

Christmas poems

Twelve Days of Christmas Anonymous
Christmas Everywhere Phillipa Brooks
A Child's Christmas Carol Christine Chaundler
How Far is it to Bethlehem Frances Chesterton
Pudding Charms Charlotte Druitt Cole
Christmas Day in the Suburbs John Cotton
Christmas Carol Eleanor Farjeon
Song Eugene Field
Christmas Day Roy Fuller
The Oxen Thomas Hardy
Four Legends about Christmas Eve Brian Levison
Carolling Around the Estate Wes Magee
Questions on Christmas Eve Wes Magee
The Carol Singers Margaret G Rhodes
A Christmas Carol Christina Rossetti
The Shepherds' Carol Clive Sanson
The Christmas Party Adeline White

Bonfire night poems

Fireworks John Cotton
Please to Remember Geoffrey Holloway
The Guy Robert L Holmes
Bonfire Jean Kenward
Please to Remember Walter de la Mare
Bonfire Night Madeline Mayne
Fireworks James Reeves
The Bonfire Anthony Thwaite

People poems

There was an Old Woman who Swallowed a Fly Anonymous
Old Mrs Thing-um-e-bob Charles Causley
The Spaceman Kay Cornish
Aunt Flo John Cotton
Herbaceous Plodd Michael Dugan
The Quarrel Eleanor Farjeon
Mrs Brown Rose Tyleman
The Dustbinmen Gregory Harrison
Esme on her Brother's Bicycle Russell Hoban
My Brother Bert Ted Hughes
Big Aunt Flo Wes Magee
Uncle James Margaret Mahy
Aunt Ermintrude Roger McGough
Uncle Terry was a Skydiver Roger McGough
When My Dad Came Home from the Sea Ian McMillan
Janitor Jeffries Peter Mortimer
My Sister Betty Gareth Owen
The Greedy Giant Laura E Richards
Sir Smasham Uppe E V Rieu
My Papa's Waltz Theodore Roethke
Grandad Michael Rosen
Father Says Michael Rosen
I am the Youngest in our House Michael Rosen
Dan the Watchman John D Sheridan
Batman John Turner
My Dad, Your Dad Kit Wright

Sea poems

The Puffin Book of Salt Sea Verse compiled Charles Causley
The Sea E M Adams
Exploring the Rock Pool John Cotton
The Ship Richard Church
The Tempest James Thomas Fields
Sea Shore John Kitching
Cargoes John Masefield
Sea Fever John Masefield
White Horses Irene F Pawsey
The Rescue Ian Serraillier
The Mermaid Alfred Lord Tennyson
The Song of the Whale Kit Wright

Spring poems

Three Days into March Moira Andrew
A Spike of Green Barbara Baker
Pippa's Song Robert Browning
The Singing Time Leonard Clark
Bluebells Olive Enoch
The Four Sweet Months Robert Herrick
Thaw Brian Jones
Our Trees in Spring E Nesbit
Apple Blossom Helen Adams Parker
Crocuses Anna M Platt
Spring from Song of Solomon
Thaw Edward Thomas
The Calendar Barbara Enphan Todd
Spring E Lucia Turnbull
Chestnut Buds Emlyn M Williams
Written in March William Wordsworth
Winter and Spring William Wordsworth
Last Snow Andrew Young

Summer poems

August Afternoon Marion Edey
August Eunice Fallon
Midsummer Night Elizabeth Gould
Rain in Summer H W Longfellow
Summer Evening Walter de la Mare
Summer is Nigh Alfred Noyes
Haytime Irene F Pawsey
June Irene F Pawsey
Poppies P A Ropes
Bed in Summer R L Stevenson
A Hot Day A S J Tessimond
August Weather Katharine Tynan
Thrushes Humbert Wolfe

Autumn poems

November John Clare
Autumn John Clare
Falling Leaves S Cook
The Fog W H Davies
November Morning Olive Dehn
Song Richard Watson Dixon
Moonlit Apples J Drinkwater
The Elm Tree Eleanor Farjeon
Something Told The Wild Geese Rachel Field
Autumn Roy Fuller
Blackberry Picking Seamus Heaney
September Mary Howitt
Autumn T E Hulme
Autumn Song Ted Hughes
Beech Leaves James Reeves
Fog Carl Sandburg
A Haiku Year Book Anthony Thwaite
On These November Evenings John Walsh

Winter poems

The North Wind Doth Blow Anonymous
Robin Redbreast William Allingham
London Snow Robert Bridges
Snow Leonard Clark
The Garden Year Sara Coleridge
The Winter Dragon Stanley Cook
Winterfield A E Coppard
The Winter Trees Clifford Dyment
Snowball Wind Aileen Fisher
Stopping by Woods on a Snowy Evening Robert Frost
January Douglas Gibson
Robin Pamela Gillian
Snow in the Suburbs Thomas Hardy
No! Thomas Hood
The Kitten in the Falling Snow James Kirkup
Week of Winter Weather Wes Magee
The Snowflake Walter de la Mare
In the Wood Eileen Mathias
Winter Morning Ogden Nash
Marbles in My Pocket Lydia Pender
Jack Frost Cecily E Pike
The Wind James Reeves
There's Snow on the Fields Christina Rossetti
Death of a Snowman Vernon Scannell
Winter the Huntsman Osbert Sitwell
Jack Frost in the Garden John P Smeeton
Whitefields James Stephens
Cat and the Weather May Sewnson
Snow Edward Thomas
Hard Frost Andrew Young

Reproducible Material

Whispers, see page 14

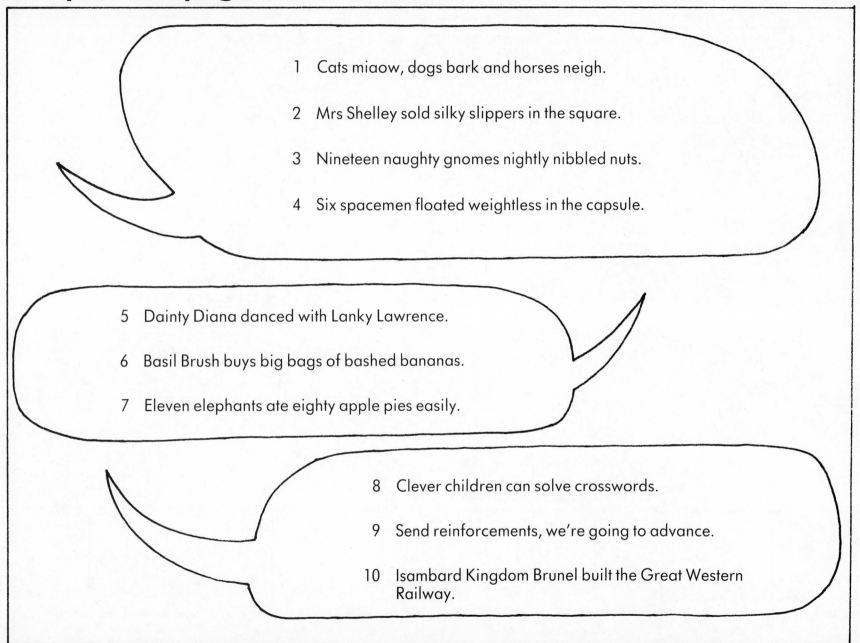

1 Cats miaow, dogs bark and horses neigh.

2 Mrs Shelley sold silky slippers in the square.

3 Nineteen naughty gnomes nightly nibbled nuts.

4 Six spacemen floated weightless in the capsule.

5 Dainty Diana danced with Lanky Lawrence.

6 Basil Brush buys big bags of bashed bananas.

7 Eleven elephants ate eighty apple pies easily.

8 Clever children can solve crosswords.

9 Send reinforcements, we're going to advance.

10 Isambard Kingdom Brunel built the Great Western Railway.

Number puzzles: totals, see page 16

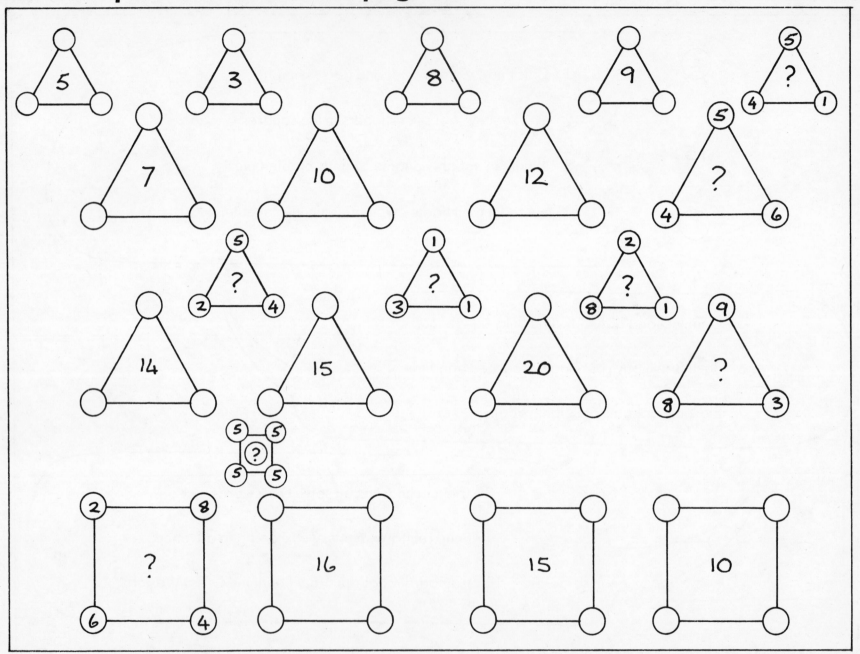

Number puzzles: sides, see page 16

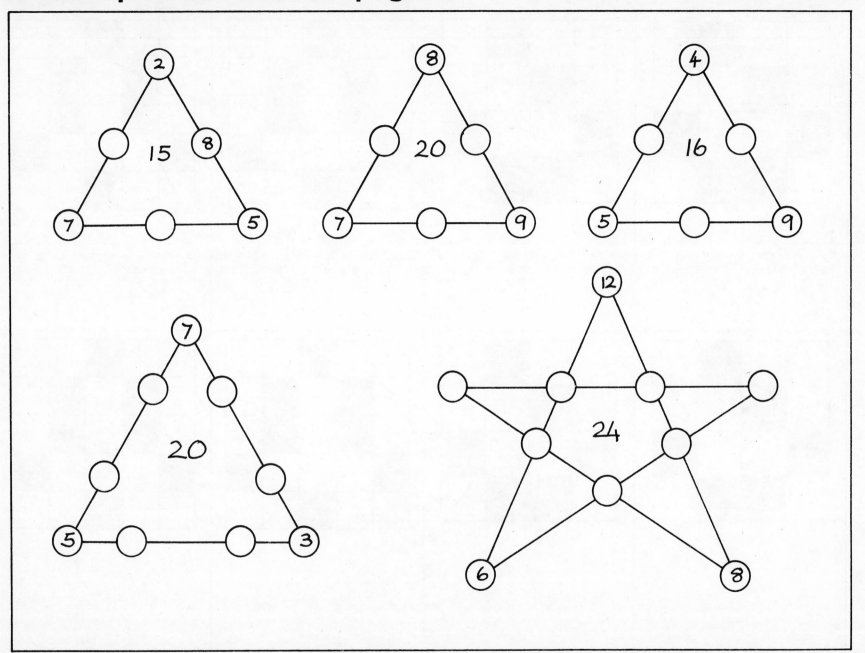

Cross numbers, see page 17

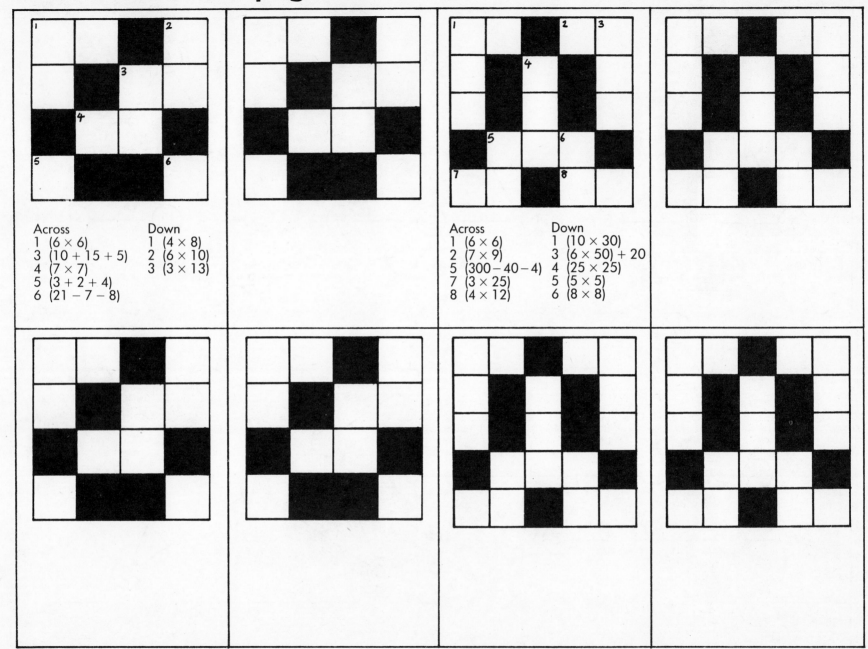

Across
1 (6 × 6)
3 (10 + 15 + 5)
4 (7 × 7)
5 (3 + 2 + 4)
6 (21 − 7 − 8)

Down
1 (4 × 8)
2 (6 × 10)
3 (3 × 13)

Across
1 (6 × 6)
2 (7 × 9)
5 (300 − 40 − 4)
7 (3 × 25)
8 (4 × 12)

Down
1 (10 × 30)
3 (6 × 50) + 20
4 (25 × 25)
5 (5 × 5)
6 (8 × 8)

Cross numbers, see page 17

Complete these crosswords.

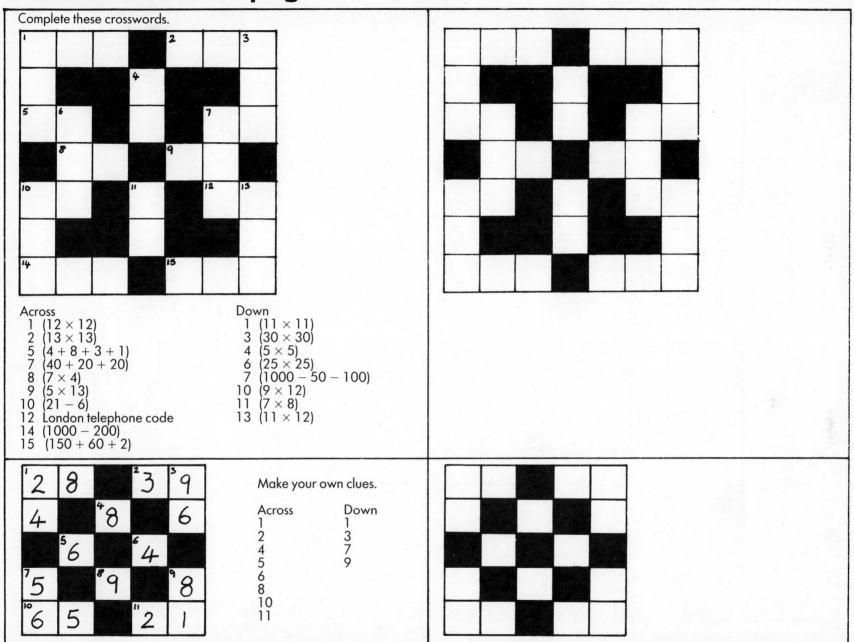

Across
1 (12 × 12)
2 (13 × 13)
5 (4 + 8 + 3 + 1)
7 (40 + 20 + 20)
8 (7 × 4)
9 (5 × 13)
10 (21 − 6)
12 London telephone code
14 (1000 − 200)
15 (150 + 60 + 2)

Down
1 (11 × 11)
3 (30 × 30)
4 (5 × 5)
6 (25 × 25)
7 (1000 − 50 − 100)
10 (9 × 12)
11 (7 × 8)
13 (11 × 12)

Make your own clues.

Across
1
2
4
5
6
8
10
11

Down
1
3
7
9

Baa baa black sheep

Have you any wool?

Yes sir, yes sir, three bags full!

One for the master,

One for the dame,

One for the little boy

Who lives down the lane.

And Jill came tumbling after.

Jack fell down and broke his crown

To fetch a pail of water.

Jack and Jill went up the hill

Little Jack Horner sat in the corner

Eating his Christmas pie.

He put in his thumb

And pulled out a plumb

And said,

"What a good boy am I!"

Mary, Mary, quite contrary,

How does your garden grow?

With silver bells

And cockle shells

And pretty maids all in a row.

Diagrams, see page 37

Anagrams, see page 38

Box 1 (Bakery):
nossec draeb slorl strat snub ABKREY snalf cutisbis unusthdog secak espi

Box 2 (Orchestra):
crahi belat Lotos sockbaoe cnebh TURNUFIRE estete sked deb oafs badurpoe breadwor

Box 3 (Clothes):
MUDRS LOVINI NOPIA EGLANTIR COSTIARHER LECOL TUFLE RHON PREMUTT PHYLONEXO BODE SABS

Box 4 (Homes):
taco heoss kossc redss thross velgos stev lolervup THELOCS urstoers timsten stanp tha rais Krist

Box 5 (Furniture):
cartree wagoblun lalvi shoeu nacavar alft SHOEM satcel gettcoa roman nismano

Box 6 (Sports):
flog ojud laboloft treckic bantell STROPS dresunor brugu blows grinac miwmisgn strad keroons wingor gixnob

Box 7 (Pets):
Rnoyme shreamt bilger nypo bartib trarop STEP shif tac ogd Rnase pyppu shore

Box 8 (Shops):
Rreamprutes rakeb tononfreccie orcreg PHOSS mengofrish moongirenr wenngesat cibotancost michest crogengrere preard

BAKERY	FURNITURE	ORCHESTRA	CLOTHES	HOMES	SPORTS	PETS	SHOPS
bread	chair	drums	pullover	bungalow	football	cat	grocer
tarts	table	piano	skirt	house	bowls	dog	greengrocer
buns	settee	triangle	dress	flat	cricket	snake	baker
flans	sofa	violin	trousers	terrace	golf	horse	confectioner
pies	bed	cello	socks	castle	judo	hamster	ironmonger
cakes	cupboard	flute	shoes	cottage	swimming	gerbil	chemist
biscuits	stool	bass	vest	manor	darts	rabbit	tobacconist
doughnuts	bench	trumpet	pants	caravan	snooker	parrot	newsagent
rolls	desk	horn	coat	mansion	boxing	monkey	fishmonger
scones	bookcase	xylophone	gloves	villa	rugby	pony	supermarket
	wardrobe	oboe	hat		rowing	puppy	draper
			mittens		rounders	fish	
			shorts		netball		
			sari				

Design a logo, see page 48

Design a logo to fit on the side of the lorry.

Is there something wrong?, see page 49

Mrs Anderson jumped out of her skin as she heard her

alarm clock start ringing. The day had arrived! Too soon,

she thought, as she put on her dressing gown and went

through to the kitchen to make some tea and toast. The

flap on the letter-box clicked. She went to collect her post,

but there was none . . . just the metal object. She collected

it, set it down on the table and went to pour the tea. Later,

after having three helpings of buttered toast with orange

marmalade and a mug of strong tea, she washed,

dressed, turned off the repeat of the news, and went

down to start the car. It was an ageing old banger. Every

cold morning it slowly ground into life. Each time, she

could never quite believe that it would make it, but this

time it did. She drove thoughtfully and carefully to work.

Hypotheses, see page 55

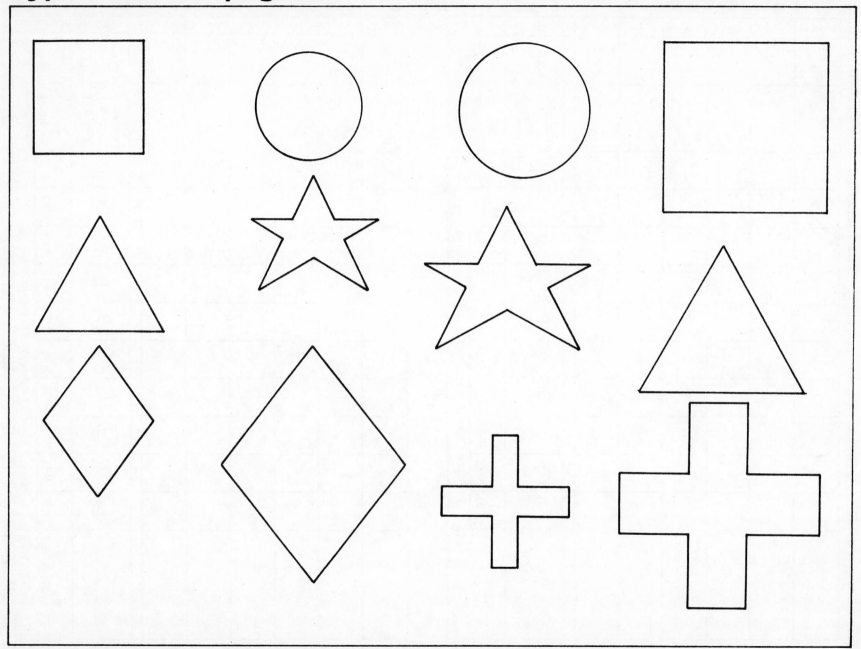

Hypotheses, see page 55

name	Number of attributes tested	Turn 1	Turn 2	Turn 3	Turn 4	Turn 5	Turn 6	Turn 7	Turn 8	Turn 9	Turn 10	score
					Number of choices per turn: ring *least*							
example Anna	3 (small red square)	6	3	12	9	6	(5)	7	(5)	4	(5)	5

name	Number of attributes tested	Turn 1	Turn 2	Turn 3	Turn 4	Turn 5	Turn 6	Turn 7	Turn 8	Turn 9	Turn 10	score
					Number of choices per turn: ring *least*							
example Stephen	4 (small yellow star)	8	11	11	9	9	8	(6)	7	(6)	(6)	6

Elf's journey, see page 56

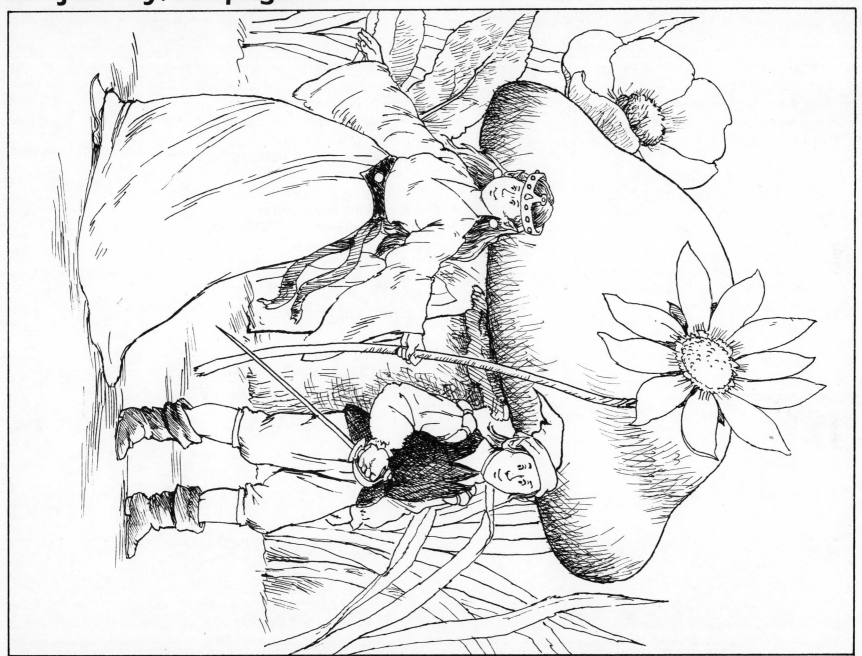

Missing words, see page 57

1 Bed in summer

In winter I get up at ....
And dress by yellow candle ....
In summer, quite the other way,
I have to go to bed by ...

I have to go to bed and see
The birds still hopping on the ....,
Or hear the grown-up peoples' ....
Still going past me in the ....

And does it not seem hard to you,
When all the sky is clear and ....
And I should like so much to ....,
To have to go to bed by ....?

R L Stevenson (1850–1894)

Author's words
night, light, day, tree, feet, street, blue, play, day.

2 Windy nights

Whenever the .... and stars are ...,
Whenever the wind is ....:,
All night long in the .... and wet,
A man goes ..... by.
Why does he ..... and .... about?

Whenever the trees are .... aloud,
And ships are ..... at sea,
By the highway low and loud,
By at the ..... goes .....
By at the .... he goes, and then
By he comes back at the ....

R L Stevenson (1850–1894)

Author's words
moon, set, high, dark, riding, out, gallop, crying, tossed, gallop, he, gallop, gallop, again.

Design a machine, see page 58

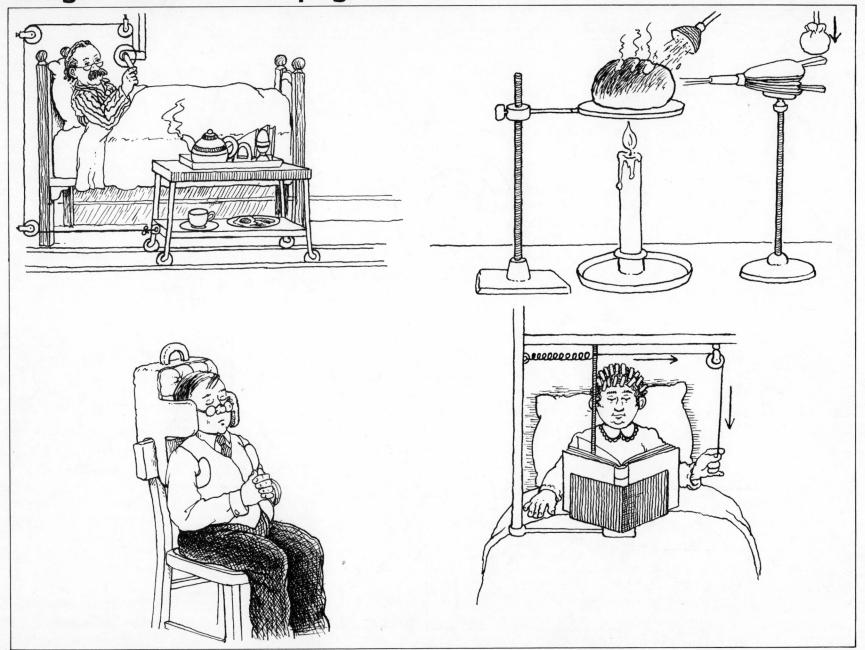

Shapes, forms and patterns, see page 60

Mistakes, see page 62

Correct these sentences (number of errors)

1   ann et a appel and a pair   (6)

2   sue ad nun   (4)

3   tadpol chanj intwo forgz   (6)

4   bobby snag veri wel butt Petre hati'd mussic leson   (12)

5   brain hoped over the crak then fel down a whole   (7)

6   stop said! Clare don't go wir out mi   (11)

7   Can I comm arsked Lee? ill bee gud   (14)

8   flys buz neer the cicling on summer daze   (8)

9   suddenley we herd a niose   (5)

10   some fingz comeing we thort!   (8)

11   Frist we tryed, hideing then we runned awey   (7)

12   We werr sune cawt buy a saylor   (7)

13   jak tolled Jil he sore a elifant stuk in a chimbley   (10)

14   cheif lawson and lady margaret wos invited to open our fate   (10)

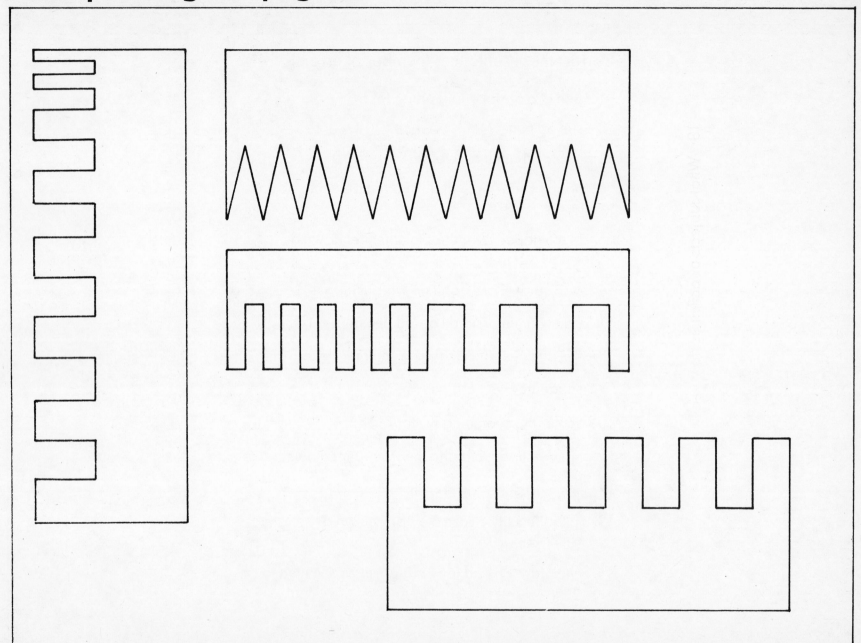

Questionnaire, see page 69

Answer these questions: Name
Date

1 Do you sit where you can see the teacher's face?
  Yes   Mostly   No

2 Do you sit a) near the teacher's desk?
             b) far from the teacher's desk?

3 Do you ask the teacher questions in the lesson?
  Sometimes   Often   Never

4 Do you always understand in lessons?
  Yes   Mostly   Sometimes   No

5 Do you day-dream at all in lessons?
  Often   Sometimes   Never

6 Do you disturb other people in class?
  Often   Sometimes   Never

7 Do other pupils disturb you in class?
  Often   Sometimes   Never

8 Do you prefer talking to your friends than working?
  Yes   Sometimes   No

9 Do you often get into trouble in class?
  Often   Sometimes   Never

10 Do you often get into trouble in the playground?
   Often   Sometimes   Never

11 Do you find the reading parts of the lesson hard?
   Yes   No

12 Do you find the writing parts of the lesson hard?
   Yes   No

13 What subjects or activities do you like best?

Friendly words, see page 70

Look for the friendly words.

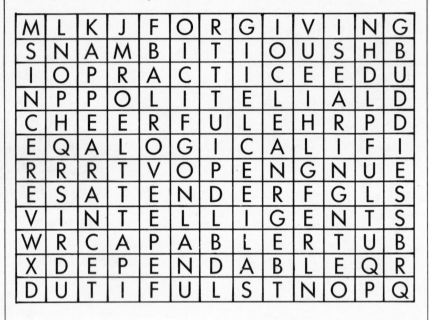

M	L	K	J	F	O	R	G	I	V	I	N	G
S	N	A	M	B	I	T	I	O	U	S	H	B
I	O	P	R	A	C	T	I	C	E	E	D	U
N	P	P	O	L	I	T	E	L	I	A	L	D
C	H	E	E	R	F	U	L	E	H	R	P	D
E	Q	A	L	O	G	I	C	A	L	I	F	I
R	R	R	T	V	O	P	E	N	G	N	U	E
E	S	A	T	E	N	D	E	R	F	G	L	S
V	I	N	T	E	L	L	I	G	E	N	T	S
W	R	C	A	P	A	B	L	E	R	T	U	B
X	D	E	P	E	N	D	A	B	L	E	Q	R
D	U	T	I	F	U	L	S	T	N	O	P	Q

Look for the friendly words.

M	L	K	J	F	O	R	G	I	V	I	N	G
S	N	A	M	B	I	T	I	O	U	S	H	B
I	O	P	R	A	C	T	I	C	E	E	D	U
N	P	P	O	L	I	T	E	L	I	A	L	D
C	H	E	E	R	F	U	L	E	H	R	P	D
E	Q	A	L	O	G	I	C	A	L	I	F	I
R	R	R	T	V	O	P	E	N	G	N	U	E
E	S	A	T	E	N	D	E	R	F	G	L	S
V	I	N	T	E	L	L	I	G	E	N	T	S
W	R	C	A	P	A	B	L	E	R	T	U	B
X	D	E	P	E	N	D	A	B	L	E	Q	R
D	U	T	I	F	U	L	S	T	N	O	P	Q

Word search, see page 70

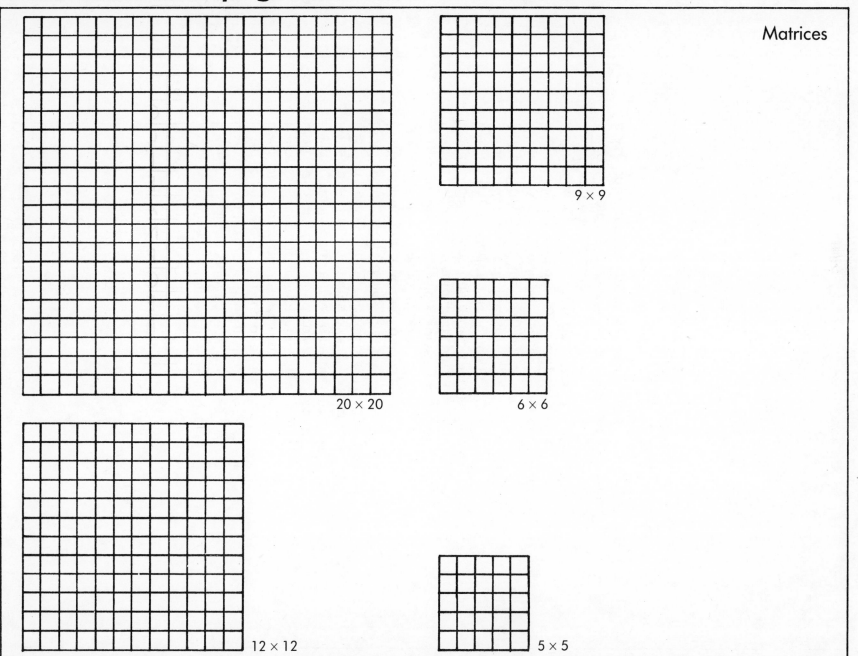

Matrices

9 × 9

20 × 20

6 × 6

12 × 12

5 × 5

Alphabet poems, see page 72

A was an Archer, and shot at a frog,
B was a Blindman, and led by a dog,
C was a Cutpurse, and lived in disgrace,   (thief)
D was a Drunkard, and had a red face,
E was an Eater, a glutton was he,
F was a Fighter and fought with a flea,
G was a Giant, and pulled down a house,
H was a Hunter, and hunted a mouse,
I was an Ill man, and hated by all,   (bad man)
K was a Knave, and he robbed great and small,
L was a Liar, and told many lies,
M was a Madman, and beat out his eyes,
N was a Nobleman, nobly born,
O was an Ostler, and stole horses' corn,
P was a Pedlar, and sold many pins,
Q was a Quarreller, and broke both his shins,
R was a Rogue, and ran about town,
S was a Sailor, a man of renown,
T was a Tailor, and knavishly bent,
U was an Usurer, took ten per cent,   (money lender),
W was a writer, and money he earned,
X was a Xenophon, prudent and learn'd,   (Xenophon
    was a famous Greek)
Y was a Yeoman, and worked for his bread,   (freeman)
Z was one Zeno the Great, but he's dead.

Anon (1700)

Secret sentences, see page 73

Error chart Pupil	Sentence No: The	teacher	placed	the	thirty-	five	little	green	marbles	on	the	side	table,	turned	round	to	the	class	and	began	the	lesson.
1																						
2																						
3																						
4																						
5																						
6																						
7																						
8																						
9																						
10																						
11																						
12																						
13																						
14																						
15																						
16																						
17																						
18																						
19																						
20																						
21																						
22																						
23																						
24																						
25																						
26																						
27																						
28																						
29																						
30																						

Words to avoid, see page 74

Change the word 'said' in these sentences. You can use a suitable word from the list or find one of your own.

Mark said he had jumped over a very high fence.

Sharma said 'I have found the lost kitten!'

'Please come for tea,' said James. 'Thank you,' said George.

Diane said she would bring her bike every day, but she never did.

'Sh-h!' said David. 'We must keep quiet.'

'Please don't play too near the road. It's dangerous,' said mother.

'Can you tell me the way to the sweet shop?' said Beverley.

'I saw the thief snatch the jewels,' said the policeman.

'Can I play football with you?' said Brian.

'No!' said some. 'Yes!' said the others.

'I've got a new football we can use,' Brian said.

'All right, you can play,' they all said.

'These biscuits are stale,' said the shopper. 'Look at the sell-by date!' she said.

'I'm most sorry, madam,' said the manager. 'It's an unfortunate mistake,' he said.

asked
shouted
replied
promised
whispered
warned
enquired
agreed
refused
cried
offered
stated
argued
pleaded
objected
claimed
declared
explained
complained
apologised

Wordsquares, see page 75

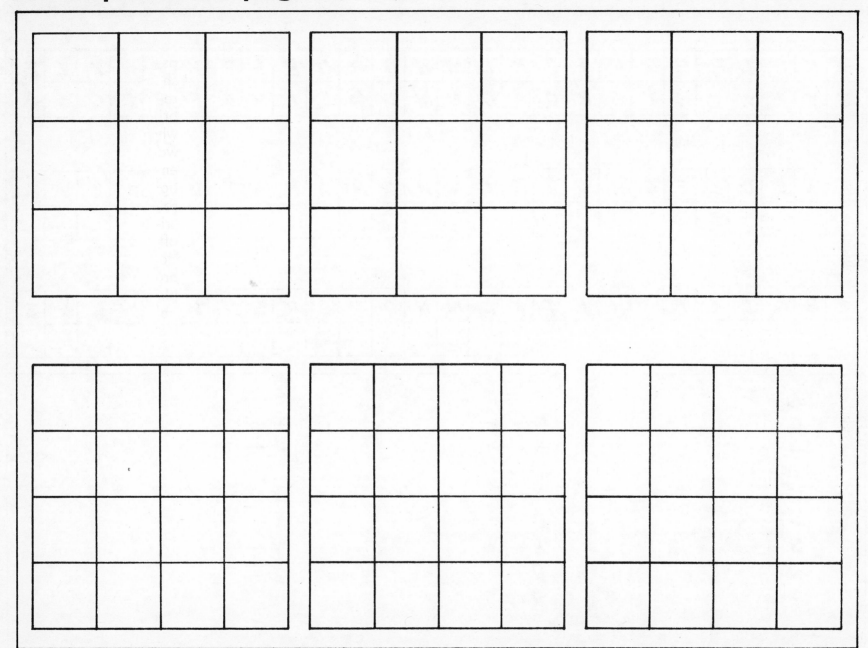

Codes, see page 76

A	B	C	D	E	F	G	H	I	J	K	L	M	N	O	P	Q	R	S	T	U	V	W	X	Y	Z
Z	Y	X	W	V	U	T	S	R	Q	P	O	N	M	L	K	J	I	H	G	F	E	D	C	B	A

A	B	C	D	E	F	G	H	I	J	K	L	M	N	O	P	Q	R	S	T	U	V	W	X	Y	Z

A	B	C	D	E	F	G	H	I	J	K	L	M	N	O	P	Q	R	S	T	U	V	W	X	Y	Z

MORSE CODE

A ·—	J ·———	S ···
B —···	K —·—	T —
C —·—·	L ·—··	U ··—
D —··	M ——	V ···—
E ·	N —·	W ·——
F ··—·	O ———	X —··—
G ——·	P ·——·	Y —·——
H ····	Q ——·—	Z ——··
I ··	R ·—·	

How many squares?, see page 77

Acknowledgements

The editors and publishers extend grateful thanks for the reuse of the following material:
British Telecom for page 34 and The Heart of England Newspapers for pages 18 and 58.

Every effort has been made to trace and acknowledge contributors. If any right has been omitted the publishers offer their apologies and will rectify this in subsequent editions following publication.

Other Bright Ideas titles

Previous titles in this series available are:

Bright Ideas Seasonal Activities
0 706 24453 2   £4.95

Bright Ideas Language Development
0 706 24452 4   £4.95

Bright Ideas Science
0 706 24455 9   £4.95

Bright Ideas Christmas Art and Craft
0 706 24454 0   £4.95

Bright Ideas Reading Activities
0 590 70535 0   £4.95

Bright Ideas Maths Activities
0 590 70534 2   £4.95

More Bright Ideas Christmas Art and Craft
0 590 70601 2   £4.95

Bright Ideas Classroom Management
0 590 70602 0   £4.95

Bright Ideas Games for PE
0 590 70690 X   £4.95

Bright Ideas Crafty Moneymakers
0 590 70689 6   £4.95

Bright Ideas Music
0 590 70700 0   £4.95

Bright Ideas Assemblies
0 590 70693 4   £4.95

Bright Ideas Writing
0 590 70701 9   £4.95

Bright Ideas Lifesavers
0 590 70694 2   £4.95

Set of any six titles   £25

Write to Scholastic Publications Ltd, Westfield Road, Southam, Leamington Spa, Warwickshire CV33 0JH. Enclose your remittance. Make cheques payable to Scholastic Publications Ltd.